PRESBYTERIAN POLITY
FOR
CHURCH LEADERS

Fourth Edition

Gwynne

Gwynne Shepherd

Email:
gigishepherd1@outlook.com

Phone:
678-787-8239

PRESBYTERIAN POLITY FOR CHURCH LEADERS

Fourth Edition

JOAN S. GRAY
and
JOYCE C. TUCKER

With a New Foreword by Cynthia Bolbach

Geneva Press
Louisville, Kentucky

© copyright John Knox Press 1986
© 1999, 2012 Joan S. Gray and Joyce C. Tucker

4th edition
Published by Geneva Press
Louisville, KY

12 13 14 15 16 17 18 19 20 21 — 10 9 8 7 6 5 4 3 2 1

Scripture quotations are from the Revised Standard Version of the Bible, copyrighted 1946, 1952, © 1971, 1973 by the Division of Christian Education of the National Council of the Churches of Christ in the U.S.A., and are used by permission.

Permission is granted from the Office of the General Assembly, Presbyterian Church (U.S.A.) to use material from the following sources: *The Constitution of the Presbyterian Church (U.S.A.)*, Part I: *Book of Confessions* and Part II: *Book of Order,* and all earlier constitutions of the predecessor denominations now part of the Presbyterian Church (U.S.A.). James E. Andrews, "We Can Be More Than We Are," Joint Committee on Presbyterian Reunion, *Resources for Studying the Plan for Reunion,* 1982. "Church Membership and Discipline" (Atlanta: Office of the Stated Clerk, Presbyterian Church in the United States, 1979). Robert Clyde Johnson, ed., *The Church and Its Changing Ministry* (Philadelphia: Office of the General Assembly, The United Presbyterian Church in the United States of America, 1961). "The Nature and Practice of Ministry" (Atlanta: Office of the Stated Clerk, Presbyterian Church in the United States, 1981). "Ordination to the Ministry of the Word" (Atlanta: Office of the Stated Clerk, Presbyterian Church in the United States, 1976).

Book Design by Sharon Adams

Library of Congress Cataloging-in-Publication Data

Gray, Joan S. (Joan Standridge)
   Presbyterian polity for church leaders / Joan S. Gray, Joyce C. Tucker; foreword by Cynthia Bolbach. — 4th ed.
      p.   cm.
   Includes bibliographical references (p.) and indexes.
   ISBN: 978-0-664-50315-4 (alk. paper)
1. Presbyterian Church (U.S.A.). Book of order. 2. Presbyterian Church (U.S.A.)—Government 3. Presbyterian Church—Government. I. Tucker, Joyce C. II. Title.
   BX8969.6.P743G73 2012
   262'.05137—dc23   2011051974

♾ The paper used in this publication meets the minimum requirements of the American National Standard for Information Sciences—Permanence of Paper for Printed Library Materials, ANSI Z39.48-1992.

*This book is dedicated
to all ruling elders of the PC(USA)
with our respect and gratitude*

CONTENTS

Contents

FOREWORD
TO THE FOURTH EDITION

The Constitution of the Presbyterian Church (U.S.A.) has always been a living document. How could it be otherwise, given that we as a church affirm *Ecclesia reformata, semper reformanda secundum verbum Dei*? That is, "The church reformed, always to be reformed, according to the Word of God" in the power of the Spirit?

The 217th General Assembly (2006) followed through on this affirmation by authorizing the establishment of a task force to propose a new Form of Government for the Presbyterian Church (U.S.A.). The General Assembly gave specific instructions to the task force: the new Form of Government was to preserve our foundational polity, it was to focus on providing leadership for local congregations as missional communities, it was to ensure that the presbytery continue as the central governmental unit of the church, and it was to provide flexibility at all levels, "granting authority while permitting governing bodies to develop the structures to carry out their respective missions." Further, the membership of the task force was to reflect the experience of the broad spectrum of the church; its members were to include at least one clerk of session, one session moderator, one new immigrant pastor, one executive/general presbyter, one stated clerk, one committee on preparation for ministry member or staff, one committee on ministry member or staff, and one member of the Advisory Committee on the Constitution.

I was privileged to be asked to be part of the task force, filling the clerk of session spot. For four years, the original task force and the task force as reconstituted by the 218th General Assembly in 2008 worked to create a Form of Government that would both preserve our overarching constitutional standards that bind us together while at the same time provide the flexibility needed to carry out effective ministry in a twenty-first-century world.

As we worked, and especially as we traveled throughout the church discussing what we were doing and seeking input, each task force member developed particular ways of explaining what we were doing. For me, as an attorney, the rationale was clear: we were returning the Form of Government to the status of what it was always intended to be—a Constitution. Since 1983, when it was approved, the Form of Government had been amended over 300 times. It had morphed from a Constitution into a "one-size–fits-all" rules manual—and "one size fits all" was no longer an effective way to operate.

The 219th General Assembly (2010) reviewed the Form of Government as proposed by the task force and, after making some changes, approved it and sent it on to the presbyteries for their vote. A majority of presbyteries voted in favor, and the new Form of Government took effect on July 10, 2011.

After reading this book I hope you will agree that the new Form of Government carries out the directives established by the 217th General Assembly. Our foundational polity has been preserved; in fact, there is now a separate section of the *Book of Order* called The Foundations of Presbyterian Polity. Breaking out the historic principles of our polity into a discrete section of the *Book of Order* emphasizes that these foundational principles apply not just to the Form of Government but to the entire *Book of Order*.

The new Form of Government is a missional polity. "Missional," unfortunately, has become somewhat of a buzz word, but I believe at its heart it means that mission happens when congregations, as nurturing communities, go out into the world in their particular corner of Christ's kingdom to proclaim the gospel message. The new Form of Government begins with congregations: G-1.0101 says that "The congregation is the church engaged in the mission of God in its particular context. The triune God gives to the congregation all the gifts of the gospel necessary to being the church. The congregation is the basic form of the church, but it is not of itself a sufficient form of the church." The congregation is where the rubber meets the road, in terms of doing mission, but we as Presbyterians also recognize that our connectional ties strengthen and undergird each of our individual congregations.

The new Form of Government provides flexibility at all levels. Sessions, presbyteries, synods, and the General Assembly—now known as councils of the church—have the responsibilities of ensuring that the Word of God is truly preached and heard, that the sacraments are rightly administered and received, and that a covenant community of disciples of Christ is nurtured. Councils have the leeway to figure out how to carry out these responsibilities most effectively and efficiently.

One of the most controversial provisions of the new Form of Government is that it permits, under certain circumstances, associate pastors or interim pastors to become the next installed pastor. Although the task force believed that, in almost all instances, allowing an interim or an associate to succeed is not the preferred option, it also took seriously the directive about flexibility. There could be the situation where the interim or associate is the absolutely right person to help a congregation carry out its mission and ministry. So the new Form of Government allows a presbytery, if it chooses, to permit associates or interims to succeed, although a three-fourths vote in favor of the succession is required of the presbytery.

The new Form of Government brings back the terms "ruling elder" and "teaching elder" to emphasize that both of these forms of ordered ministry share equally in the leadership of our church. I believe the role of ruling elders has been seriously diminished over the past thirty years—far too often, serving on a session as a ruling elder has been equated to serving on a nonprofit board of directors. In fact, ruling elders have the awesome, and awe-filled, task of discerning and measuring a congregation's fidelity to the Word of God. We need to reclaim the role of the ruling elder in the life of our church.

The Presbyterian Church (U.S.A.) is currently in the midst of retooling itself, changing from the bureaucratic, corporate model that was adopted in the middle of the twentieth century into a leaner, more flexible style that better reflects the realities that confront us in the twenty-first century. The corporate organizational style is premised on a denomination that is flush with resources and members. We are no longer flush with members or with resources. Let me be clear, however: this diminution of members and resources does not mean that we are dying. The appropriate test of whether we are dying is not our number of members or the amount of our financial resources but whether we are proclaiming the gospel authentically.

I believe we are proclaiming the gospel authentically. I also believe, however, that the corporate model inhibits us from proclaiming it as effectively as possible. The new Form of Government is not a panacea; it will not magically transform us from the black-and-white television set that is our current corporate model into the flat-screen, high-definition set that we need to do ministry at this time and in this place. But it does provide the mind-set that we need to carry out the transformation from black and white to HD.

The new Form of Government is to be embraced, not feared. I'm grateful to Joan Gray and Joyce Tucker for updating their classic book about Presbyterian polity so that all Presbyterians can understand the new Form of Government and so that we all can live into it and use its full potential for transforming our life and work together.

Cynthia Bolbach
Moderator, 219th General Assembly (2010)

FOREWORD
TO THE THIRD EDITION

Why are things in the church the way they are and not some other way? This book seeks not only to describe the government of the Presbyterian Church but also to explain some of the reasons for things being as they are. In addition to history, tradition, and convenience, there are also reasons that grow out of our understanding of the nature of the Christian faith. Certain fundamental convictions derived from the reading of Scripture have helped to shape the *Book of Order* and the Presbyterian Church into what they are today.

Is this form of government taught in Scripture? Almost all churches look to Scripture to justify their particular forms and orders. Rather than trying to use Scripture to justify the particular provisions or even the ordered ministries of the church, it is more helpful to observe the ways in which some of the fundamental affirmations of the Reformed faith find expression in our church's government. It is difficult to decide which came first, theological understanding or form of government. In Calvin's own writing and work these two were very closely related. The development of this new way of being the church called "Reformed" can scarcely be separated from the development of a new system of theological reflection. Indeed, we can see influence flowing both ways: (*a*) Particular affirmations of faith are lived out in church order, and (*b*) the lived experience of Reformed Christians has shaped the theological stance. In what follows, I will suggest several convictions about God and the Christian life that find clear expression in the Presbyterian form of government. Others could have been chosen or added, but these form the core of a theological answer to the question: Why are things in the Presbyterian Church the way they are?

The Covenant. The idea of the covenant has long influenced the Reformed way of viewing God and God's relationship with humanity. Out of their conviction that what God began with Israel God completed in Jesus Christ, Calvin and others found in the covenants of the Old Testament the foundation for the Christian life. The covenant image was so powerful because it reminded Calvin that initiative in salvation, as in creation, lay entirely with God: It was *God* who called Israel, *God* who chose Abraham and Sarah, *God* who gave the law through Moses to the people. Each act was an act of grace, not done because any had deserved it; in each case it was God who sought out people with whom to have a relationship.

Such a notion of the primacy of divine initiative and grace lies at the heart of the Reformed understanding of the church. We do not "join" the church of our choosing; rather, we are called by God into relationship. In the language of faith, we are sought before we ourselves find. It is this conviction that undergirds the Reformed emphasis on "infant" baptism. As God made covenant with Abraham and Sarah and their offspring, so God elects or chooses us before we are conscious that there is a God to choose. As church members, then, we do not depend on our agreement with one another in matters of belief or practice to keep us together. We are together because we believe that God has called each of us and that therefore we can and should live together.

This conviction of being called to life together is the second aspect of the covenant theme. The covenants of the Old Testament created the people of Israel; in the New Testament the covenant sealed in the blood of Christ created the church. Individuals are called of God, but they are always called *into* community with one another. However much we would prefer to go it alone, the Christian life is always life together. While this is a conviction shared by almost all Christians, it has led Reformed Christians into particular ways of ordering church life.

Not infrequently you will hear people complain about the never-ending use of committees in the Presbyterian Church; frustrated members and pastors sometimes say, "If you want something done right, do it yourself." The notion that we are called to *be* together has led Presbyterians to conclude that this is how we should make decisions: not independently or unilaterally, but together. This is as true within the life of a local congregation as it is for the denomination as a whole. Decisions are shared among the various members or councils for the good of the whole, because *together* we are the body of Christ.

The Law. As noted above, one of the highlights of God's covenant making with Israel was the gift of the law. The Ten Commandments and the laws that flowed from them gave form or shape to the nation of Israel. The law made life together just, humane, and possible. To be sure, the law was abused: not only was it violated, but also the keeping of the law was used to assure individuals of their worthiness or righteousness. Calvin joined Luther in asserting that human beings were made righteous (or set in right relationship with God) by God's grace alone and not by any human works, even by keeping God's law. Calvin, however, retained a rather more positive view of the law itself than did Luther. He saw it as a gift of grace that could provide an orderly means for people to live together under God. The order of law provided the environment in which people could grow together in grace.

Since an ordered life is crucial for growth, it is small wonder that various forms of government and order have played such a central place in the life of Reformed or Presbyterian churches. The *Book of Order* is *not* a manual of operations. It is a way of making Christian life in community possible. (It is not the only way, to be sure, but one that generations have found conducive to the nurture of faith.) *The Book of Order* is to be studied and learned by those who are leaders in the church because of their responsibility to guide and guard that life together.

Included in the *Book of Order* are the Rules of Discipline. These are procedures to be followed when there is serious difficulty in the life of the church. The intention of these regulations, however, must be carefully noted: discipline in the church is to be exercised for "building up the body of Christ, not for destroying it, for redeeming, not for punishing" [D-1.0102]. The same could be said of the entire form of government: these provisions are gifts that can enable orderly and peaceful life together.

Sin. As Luther and Calvin both pointed out, one of the functions of the law of God was to convict humanity of its sin. Judged by that standard of righteousness, no one is innocent. This conviction of the pervasiveness of sin even in the lives of believers stands at the heart of the Reformed faith. Many who see this as a gloomy doctrine fail to recognize that it must always be held alongside the unshakable conviction that we *have been justified* by the redemptive work of God in Christ. But on this side of the fulfillment of the kingdom, the world, believers and unbelievers alike, will be subject to the consequences of human sin.

Such a theological affirmation has led to two convictions about the church and decision making that we experience every day as Presbyterians. First, the Reformers assumed that not even the church was immune from the effects of human sin. Because the church was made up of human beings and because all humans have sinned and fallen short of the glory of God, the Reformers held that it could and did make errors of judgment and worse. The Reformation itself was an attempt precisely to reform and purify the church of its more obvious abuses of ecclesiastical and political power. Those same Reformers were not so naive as to assume that the reformed church would not become subject to similar abuses in time. Thus came the motto first used in the Dutch Reformed Church: *Ecclesia reformata, semper reformanda*—the church reformed, always to be reformed. This is a commitment to continual self-examination, to the recognition that good policies do not always produce good results and that "new occasions teach new duties." Reformations are never easy, and change always brings a certain amount of conflict. The *Book of Order* is one means of ordering change and conflict so that minority views are always heard and so that petitions to amend or to redress grievance can always be presented in a civil manner. These procedures for change allow the church to be reformed under the leading of God in each new day.

The second implication of the doctrine of human sinfulness relates to the corporate nature of decision making discussed above. Because it is assumed that all persons will be subject to personal and selfish interest, it is a hallmark of the Presbyterian order that power and decision making are never vested in individuals acting alone. The powers of a pastor acting alone are severely restricted; the power and authority in a Presbyterian congregation rest with the session of which the pastor is a member. The reason that Presbyterians have always been skeptical about the office of bishop is the potential abuse that could result from vesting too much authority in one person. In contrast the presbytery is often called the "corporate bishop," because it is a representative body of constituent congregations and ministers that makes decisions concerning the life and mission of the church in a given area. The conviction that sin is both real and inevitable has led Reformed Christians to the conclusion that the decisions that we make together will most often be better than the decisions that any one of us could make individually.

Called to Serve. Having stressed the reality of human sin, Presbyterians have not found this sufficient reason for withdrawing from the world or from relations with others. Indeed, the effect of the justifying grace of God is precisely to lead persons into relationship with one another and into mission in the world. Those whom God has called have been given grace to amend their lives and the responsibility to serve God and others. Whether in sending evangelists to Korea or Zaire, sharing the poverty of Native Americans on various reservations, or building schools and colleges across the nation, Presbyterians have felt called to act out their faith in God's grace in the world around them. This has sometimes led to conflict in the church: What are the priorities for mission? Where does service end and political action begin? How much money should be spent for what?

The Presbyterian system of government is intended not only to enable life together in the church but also to facilitate the church's mission in the world. Each council has a unique role to play in determining the overall mission of the church as well as in developing its own form of service in the particular place in which it finds itself. Because of the corporate nature of the church, what is done by one is done in the name of all. This has led, to be sure, to significant differences of opinion in the church, but it has also enabled the church to act and speak as one in a world hungry for unity.

The Sovereignty of God. At its heart, any theological question is a matter of our understanding of God. Who God is and how we understand God's self-revelation is *the* issue from which all other affirmations of faith flow. For the Reformed tradition, God's sovereignty and, in particular, the sovereign nature of God's grace have seemed most compelling. Sovereignty is a political concept, born in the days when power in the human world was exercised by rulers acting more or less independently and often with unchecked authority. Applied to God, the concept of sovereignty recognizes that God was not under any compulsion but, rather, freely chose to create the world and redeem humankind. Even more, God has created the world and saves individuals without assistance, not even from the individuals concerned.

If God is thus sovereign over both the creation and human destiny, God is likewise sovereign over the church. All authority in the church rightly belongs to God, working through the Holy Spirit; all other authority exercised by persons and groups is derivative. All Christians affirm, of course, that Christ is the head of the church, which is the body of Christ. For Presbyterians this affirmation implies that we can invest in no person or church council the kind of absolute authority or honor that belongs to God alone. Along with the conviction that the church, because it is human, will err, this view of God's sovereignty has led to healthy self-criticism and a general reluctance on the part of church leaders to assume that they are speaking for God.

Another implication of this notion of God's sovereignty is the principle that "God alone is Lord of the conscience" (Westminster Confession of Faith, XXII, 6.109). God alone, and not any church council or nation or any other human authority, has claim on complete human obedience. There are several things that this affirmation does *not* mean. It does not mean that we do not owe allegiance and loyalty to various human institutions; it does not mean that we are not subject to one another in the Lord; it does not mean that to be a Christian is to go off by oneself with Jesus, acting and believing as one wishes. The Christian faith is still to be lived in community with others, where the opinions of others and the will of the majority are to be respected.

The notion of God's sovereignty over human conscience affirms that God, as in days of old, continues to make God's will known directly to particular persons and communities of faith. The conviction that God's will is not confined to the traditions of the church, or even to traditional interpretations of Scripture, has far-reaching consequences. The decision by the Presbyterian Church to ordain women was the result of the conscience of some members convincing the whole church that a traditional interpretation of Scripture was in error and that, in fact, God does call both women and men to service and leadership in the church. Similarly, the conviction that God alone is authoritative in human conscience has led Reformed Christians to defy and/or seek to reform human governments when those governments claimed absolute authority or when their laws compelled Christians to act unjustly (The Theological Declaration of Barmen is an example of the first; the stand of the church on the matters of slavery and sanctuary for refugees may be cited as examples of the second).

The sovereignty of God is finally an affirmation of the sovereignty of God's grace. The love, compassion, and mercy of God for humanity can never be frustrated and have already triumphed in the death and resurrection of Christ. In that alone is our hope—for ourselves, for this world, and for the Presbyterian Church. Confidence in the sovereign grace of God enables us to live together and work out our differences while we recall that the hope of the world does not rest on our shoulders. The government and discipline of the Presbyterian Church have at times become demonic: Procedures have taken precedence over people; supposed purity has led to schism and rejection of each other; order has been used as a club and not a guide. The only thing that can save Presbyterians from confusing the *Book of Order* with God is grace. Only a constant recollection of who made us and brought us together, only the continual affirmation that it is mercy alone by which we live, enable us to make of our form of government what it is: a way of being the church by the grace of God.

Which came first, the order or the theology? That's hard to tell. As Calvin wrote his first rules of discipline he continued to refine his theology. It is the experience of Reformed Christians living in the world under the Word of God that has brought both doctrine and order to the present day. The *Book of Order* is not finished yet, and neither is our task of being faithful to God.

Cynthia M. Campbell
President Emerita, McCormick Theological Seminary
Chicago, Illinois

ACKNOWLEDGMENTS

As the saying goes, in the writing of this book we have drunk from wells we did not dig. We are deeply indebted to all the people involved in the new Form of Government project. We are thankful to the task force members for their work on behalf of the whole church, and for all the wonderful reference materials they provided to help us all get up to speed on the new system and give us insight into their process in creating it. We are thankful to those at Geneva Press who believed that this book should go forward and assisted us in producing the fourth edition. We owe a deep debt of gratitude to the Rev. Dr. Cynthia Campbell, President Emerita of McCormick Seminary, for allowing us to continue to use her excellent theological foreword to the third edition of this book. Ruling Elder Cynthia Bolbach, Moderator of the 219th General Assembly of the PC(USA) and co-moderator of the task force that produced the current Form of Government and Fundamental Principles of Presbyterian Polity, was kind enough to write the foreword for this edition.

Most of all we wish to give our deepest thanks to Ms. Camille Josey, our researcher for this project. Camille put the full measure of her superb polity brain and her research and computer skills behind this revision. Without her tireless work it may never have been finished and certainly would not have appeared in a timely fashion.

INTRODUCTION

"Something old, something new" could very well be a descriptive subtitle for the *Book of Order*'s new Foundations of Presbyterian Polity and Form of Government. Those who read them will find many things that sound very familiar. Much of the new Foundations of Presbyterian Polity section as well as the new Form of Government use the same wording as their predecessors. The important characteristic principles are still in place. What has changed is that there is now much more freedom for councils and congregations to do things in the way that best further their mission instead of hampering it. While the principles are still the same, some of the mandatory provisions of the former Form of Government have been stripped away. This enables churches and councils to experiment, create new things, and generally engage in a process of trial and error to the end that their structures best suit their mission. In church life one size does not fit all, and after many years of a one-size-fits-all polity, it is refreshing to have new options.

As we think about the changes in the Form of Government what comes to mind is the term "white space." This term comes from the visual arts field. It refers to the portion of a page [of whatever color] without words, graphics, or photographs. White space is an important part of a design; it provides rest to the eye, removes clutter, and gives clarity to what it surrounds. White space allows the viewer to enter into the text or design with more freedom. It is spare and inviting.

The new Form of Government with its lean framework creates white space in our polity. It helps us see the essentials more clearly. It gives us the freedom to create new things in our common life. Going from a densely constructed Form of Government with much mandatory language to one that is elegantly lean does, however, present challenges.

Freedom can be scary. One challenge is learning some new terms. One of these new terms to note is "by rule." This simply means that each council will decide how to do certain things and record it as the rule of future proceedings. This keeps them from having to decide everything anew at each meeting. What used to be called "governing bodies" are now "councils." The terms "higher councils" and "more-inclusive councils" refer to the same things and are used interchangeably in this book.

The transition into the current Form of Government may also be challenging because things that used to be specified in the pre-2011 Form of

Government are now left up to the various councils to decide. For instance, it formerly was mandatory that presbyteries review the minutes of sessions annually. This is no longer specified. Instead the review and control functions of councils are expressed, and each council above the session will need to decide how best to fulfill it. This is the pattern for much of the current Form of Government. Functions are specified; forms are not.

Many congregations that did not have written bylaws or operational guidelines before will need to write them now. The current Form of Government no longer specifies such things as what constitutes adequate notice for special meetings. As congregations and other councils write their bylaws and work to live into this new polity, the stated clerks of the more-inclusive councils will be excellent resources.

"For freedom Christ has set us free!" Freedom that is used to do mission more effectively by the leading of the Holy Spirit is a great thing. We live in a world that desperately needs what only the disciples of Jesus Christ can give. The challenges of our day require new forms and new strategies. This Form of Government gives us the freedom to craft new ways of doing things to reach a new generation for Christ. It may take a good bit of work to get used to all this white space. Change is almost always hard. But once we begin to live into our new freedom we may find the Holy Spirit meeting and empowering us for all kinds of Godly adventures in mission.

This book is written from the perspective of the local congregation. It focuses on those aspects of Presbyterian polity that ordained leaders of a particular church—ruling elders, deacons, and teaching elders—should know to carry out their ministry. It is the hope of the authors that it will prove useful to leaders in training classes and continuing education and perhaps to theological school students as they prepare for service in congregations. While we have tried to suggest the outlines of Presbyterian polity as expressed in the *Book of Order* of the Presbyterian Church (U.S.A.), this volume it not an exhaustive handbook with answers for every question. It is intended, instead, to entice leaders into a deeper study of the book itself.

References to the *Book of Order* or quotes from it are designated throughout the text by section numbers. For example, in the citation G-3.0104, "G" refers to the Form of Government, "3" locates the reference in the third chapter, and ".0104" refers to a particular section. In the Directory for Worship and Rules of Discipline the designation ".0000" refers to the entire chapter. For example, W-5.0000 refers to the entire fifth chapter of the Directory for Worship. References beginning with the letter "F" can be found in the Foundations of Presbyterian Polity, "W" references can be found in the Directory for Worship, and those with the letter "D" in the Rules of Discipline. The *Book of Order* contains a large number of cross-references within the text of particular sections. For this reason, to avoid confusion, the cross-references will be enclosed by parentheses and the authors' citations from the *Book of Order* will be in brackets.

In the next years as we live into the new Form of Government, there will probably be much change in our constitutional documents. The information in this book is intended to be correct through July 10, 2011. This is the date that the amendments approved by the 219th General Assembly and then approved by a majority of the presbyteries took effect. Readers should be aware, however, that there are changes, sometimes major ones, made in the *Book of Order* every other year. Every ordained leader should have a copy of the most recent edition and check it for new developments.

In this book the terms "teaching elder" and "ruling elder" are reintroduced into our form of government. These words will be very familiar to some and unfamiliar to others. For a while some of us may get the two confused. They both refer to persons in the ordered ministry of the church. While "minister of the Word and Sacrament" [G-2.0501] and "pastor" are still quite acceptable terms, the term "teaching elder" puts the focus on the theological functions of the clergy. The term "ruling elder" puts the focus on the governance functions of the elder. Teaching elders and ruling elders bring their special gifts together in the session and other councils to guide the church. Teaching elders are those who have met all the requirements and gone through the trials to be ordained in the ministry of the Word and Sacrament. Ruling elders are elders of the church who are elected by the congregation from among its members to exercise governance in the church. In this book we use the terms "teaching elder," "pastor," and "minister" interchangeably as each seems most appropriate to the context.

Churches come in all sizes and shapes, and some particulars of church government vary depending on the complexity of each organization. We have tried to sketch the boundaries and outline the general pattern of Presbyterian polity, hoping that within these boundaries leaders will find creative ways to make the system work in their own church. All the information given here may not apply to every congregation at a given time, but what is included is here because it may prove useful to some churches in certain circumstances.

Our polity is created to run on trust. It is predicated on the notion that disciples of Jesus Christ come together to seek the will of God with good will, Christian humility, and forbearance. The system was never meant to be a tight system of laws that kept us from ever having to think things through or engage in discernment. One of the best investments we can make in the years ahead is to build trust in our congregations, sessions, and higher councils.

Finally, while this is a book tightly focused on the polity of our church, knowing polity is only a means to an end. The end is that, above all else, members of councils should seek God's will themselves and lead the whole church in that path. This is the highest and most important function of church leaders. Ruling elders, deacons, and teaching elders are spiritual leaders. In addition to knowing polity and theology, they must be versed in Scripture, be fervent and frequent in prayer, and be practicing the time-tested spiritual disciplines of the faith. Without these things at the core of a leader's life, polity is empty; it may even become destructive.

We offer this book with thanks for the privilege of serving as officers in the Presbyterian Church (U.S.A.) and in the hope that in some small way it may be used to give glory to God and to build up the church of Jesus Christ.

Chapter One

A POLITY
FOR
THE CHURCH

Jill McLauren was looking over a list of classes for adults being offered by her church. Among the listings was a course called "Presbyterian Church Polity." "Polity," she mused. "I wonder what that is."

The session of Crosslake Presbyterian Church had spent more than an hour debating whether to permit persons to smoke on the church grounds. As time for adjournment drew near and no consensus was in sight, one of the ruling elders moved that the question be put to the congregation for a vote. The moderator ruled the motion out of order, but several ruling elders objected. "We have not been able to come to agreement about this, so why not let the congregation decide?"

The business meeting of the session of Springs Presbyterian Church was winding down. Stan Wasylkiv had just been elected commissioner to an upcoming meeting of presbytery. At this meeting several controversial issues were going to be debated. When the agenda was completed, the moderator asked for a motion to adjourn. "Wait a minute!" said a ruling elder. "We haven't given Stan any instructions about how he should vote at the presbytery meeting. As our delegate he needs to know what we want him to do."

What Is Polity?

Although the church was founded by Jesus Christ and is uniquely spiritual in character, it is also a human organization. Organizations require structure and a system of agreed-upon rules in order to carry out their tasks. Every organized group functions under rules or bylaws of some sort, even though they may be informal and unwritten. The larger the organization and the more complex its task, the more important it is that its structure and rules be efficient and flexible.

The system of rules that governs a church is called its "polity." While there is an almost endless variety of belief and practice among Christian churches today, church polities can be roughly divided into three basic kinds. These are congregational, episcopal, and presbyterian.

Congregational Polity. Direct government of the church by the people who make up the congregation characterizes the congregational style of polity. The final authority on any question is the vote of a majority of the members of that particular congregation. Each local church is autonomous; it functions without any outside control. No other church body can tell a church with this kind of polity what to do or to believe. Each congregation has its own bylaws and is sovereign in dealing with matters within its fellowship.

While churches of this kind may belong to certain associations or conventions made up of like-minded congregations, they still guard their independence jealously. It has been said, for instance, that while there are many Baptist churches (holding generally recognized Baptist doctrine), there is no Baptist Church. Congregations may cooperate to support a theological seminary or send missionaries to foreign countries, but their unity is strictly functional and voluntary.

Congregational polity comes close to being pure democracy in action. Frequent meetings of the congregation are held in which the business of the church is transacted. The congregation votes on whether or not to receive new members and sets the conditions for their membership. The congregation hires and fires the minister and other staff members. The congregation approves the church budget and votes on significant unbudgeted expenses. All matters of policy are decided by the congregation. Most churches with congregational polity do have a board of laypeople (often called deacons) who administer the will of the congregation and make recommendations to it, but finally it is the congregation that governs the life of the church.

Adherents to congregational polity point to primitive Christianity as their model. During the days of the apostles and for some time afterward, there was little or no formal connection between congregations. Individually they elected their own officers, ran their own affairs by the vote of the members, and engaged only in the very loosest sort of association with other churches. The personal and written contacts with the apostles and a common faith in the risen Christ held these early congregations together. Congregational church government also rests on the belief that the influence of the Holy Spirit shows itself in the church primarily through the views and opinions of individual members speaking within the context of the particular congregation. What one congregation hears the Spirit saying to it is not necessarily what is being heard by another; therefore, each reserves the right to do what seems appropriate in its own situation. Almost without exception all Baptist churches have a congregational form of polity. Other churches that are congregational to a greater or lesser degree are the Disciples of Christ, the United Church of Christ, and various Pentecostal denominations.

Episcopal Polity. This form of church government takes its name from the Greek word for bishop: *episkopos*, literally "shepherd." While congregational polity gives virtually all authority to the congregation, in episcopal polity power is lodged in the highest-ranking bishop and is delegated downward through the clergy.

One important facet of episcopal polity is the doctrine of "apostolic succession." Simply stated, this is the belief that those who are ordained as clergy stand in an unbroken line of authority going back to Jesus and the apostles. Christ empowered his apostles to carry on the ministry and teaching of the church. It is this power, derived from the church's founder, that the bishops exercise. According to this polity, those who stand in this unbroken line of orthodoxy have been given the authority to govern in the church.

Various rankings of clergy are also a facet of the episcopal system. In some churches, the office of bishop may be the only rank above that of parish clergy. A bishop is in authority over a number of congregations in a given area, often called a diocese. In other churches, such as the Roman Catholic Church, there are numerous ranks, including those of bishop, archbishop, cardinal, and pope. Power is apportioned according to rank in the church, with some functions also being reserved for certain officers. Bishops ordain clergy, for example. This apportionment of power and function provides for control of and uniformity among the various congregations. While there may be some latitude for local preferences, for the most part the liturgy, doctrine, and practice of congregations with strict episcopal polity vary little within the denomination.

More Christians by far belong to churches holding to some form of episcopal polity than belong to either congregational or presbyterian polities. Included in their number are the Roman Catholic Church and the Orthodox churches. The Methodist, Wesleyan, and Anglican churches depart in a number of ways from strict episcopal polity, especially in giving more authority to laypersons. Their use of the office of bishop, however, qualifies them for inclusion in this category.

Presbyterian Polity. The name of our church, "Presbyterian," refers not to our doctrine or beliefs but also to how we govern ourselves. Presbyterian polity takes its name from the Greek word *presbuteros*, meaning one having great age. "Presbyter," an English word derived from this Greek term, refers both to teaching and ruling elders as leaders in the church. Each of our congregations is governed by a group of presbyters elected by the congregation and known as the session.

Presbyterians recognize that the Scriptures do not contain a detailed plan for church government; in spite of this, Presbyterians (along with other Christian churches) have always sought to base their polity on principles found in the Bible. The *Book of Order* states that "Scripture teaches us of Christ's will for the Church, which is to be obeyed" [F-1.0203].

In keeping with this idea, the ordered ministries of our church—presbyter (ruling and teaching elders) and deacons—are ones for which there is clear precedent in Scripture. Acts 6:1–6 tells of the origin of an ordered ministry like that of deacon to meet a need in the early church. The Scripture establishes this ministry as one of service to those in need.

The New Testament also shows evidence of the use of the ordered ministry of presbyter or elder. The writer of 1 Timothy gives detailed instructions as to the character and qualifications of those who would aspire to this role (1 Tim. 3:1–7; 5:17–22). The book of James instructs those who are sick in the church to call the elders to pray for them (Jas. 5:14). First Peter 5:1–10 is an exhortation to the elders in several churches in Asia. Acts 14:23 speaks of Paul and Barnabas ordaining "elders for them in every church, with prayer and fasting."

Presbyterians believe that the New Testament uses the words "bishop" and "elder" to refer to the same ordered ministry. This can be seen in Titus 1:5 and 1:7, as well as in Acts 20:17, 28.[1] Thus, there is no hierarchy of presbyters in the Presbyterian Church; teaching and ruling elders differ only in the functions they are called to perform. When functioning together in councils, they are equals. We do not have individuals serving under the title of bishop in our denomination. At meetings of the church councils, all presbyters stand on the same footing, and decisions are made by majority vote of the whole body. Even those elected to be officers of governing bodies, moderators and clerks, have no individual authority outside the body. Their only power is that which has been assigned to them for their term of office by the council that elected them.

Another principle of our polity derived from Scripture is that power within the church is to be exercised by groups of leaders rather than individuals. Both Old and New Testaments refer to gatherings of leaders that exercised government over the people (Deut. 27:1; 2 Sam. 5:3; Acts 15:6).[2] We believe that the Holy Spirit speaks most clearly on matters of government through the prayerful deliberations of groups of presbyters. While the decisions of groups are also likely to be fallible, Presbyterian polity holds that groups are generally less likely to fall into error than are individuals. Therefore most decisions in our church are made by ordained leaders organized into groups called *councils*.

Fundamentals of Presbyterian Polity

Presbyterian churches are found the world over, and the details of their polity differ somewhat to accommodate differences in culture and circumstance. There are, however, at least three fundamental characteristics without which a system of church government could hardly be called presbyterian. Ours is a polity that is representative, constitutional, and relational.

Representative. The Presbyterian Church (U.S.A.) is governed by groups of presbyters elected by the people. One of the rights of the Presbyterian congregation is that of electing its own installed leaders [G-2.0102]. Therefore, no higher council can instruct a congregation to install a particular man or woman in a permanent ordered ministry against its will. This power is exercised under the oversight of the session and the presbytery, and in certain cases the session or presbytery can exercise a "veto power" over the congregation's decisions. If the congregation elects a ruling elder who cannot pass the ordination examination given by the session or one whom the session finds morally unacceptable, the session can refuse to ordain that person. Also the congregation votes to call a pastor and establishes the pastor's terms of call, but the presbytery may refuse to approve either the person or the terms of call if it finds them unacceptable. This system of government by leaders duly elected by the people is a primary difference between our polity and congregational or episcopal polity.

The congregation in Presbyterian churches governs in ways that are strictly limited. The congregation elects leaders who govern the church. These leaders, serving as the session, are responsible for making most decisions relating to the congregation's life and welfare. This is why, as in the situation outlined at the beginning of the chapter, it would not be advisable for the congregation to vote on whether smoking should be permitted on church property. This is a matter of policy relating to the use of church property, and responsibility for making such policies rests with the session [G-3.0201c].

Leaders elected by congregations or councils to serve in more-inclusive councils cannot be told how to vote. Our leaders must be free to listen for the word of Christ to his church. As *commissioners*, therefore, they are independent decision makers, and they cannot be bound to vote according to the wishes of those who elected them. A meeting of commissioners is a deliberative body open to the give-and-take of discussion and to the free working of the Holy Spirit. In contrast, those elected in settings outside the Presbyterian Church to serve as *delegates* to meetings may be instructed beforehand and are then obligated to act in accordance with their instructions. The outcome of a question before a meeting of delegates, say a political convention, may be decided in advance, because delegates generally have no option except to vote as they have been instructed.

Our church does not elect such delegates to serve in councils. Presbyters are to seek the will of Christ for the church. They must not be mirrors reflecting only the will of the people [F-3.0204]. They are finally responsible, not to the congregation, but to Christ, for the decisions they make.

Constitutional. Our church has a Constitution that seeks to put our beliefs and polity into writing. This Constitution has two parts: the *Book of Confessions* and the *Book of Order* [F-3.04].

A confession, or creed, is an authoritative expression of the Christian faith, or some part of it, expressed by Christians using the language of their own day.

> In these statements the church declares to its members and to the world
>> who and what it is,
>
>> what it believes, and
>
>> what it resolves to do.
>
> These statements identify the church as a community of people known by its convictions as well as by its actions. They guide the church in its study and interpretation of the Scriptures; they summarize the essence of Reformed Christian tradition; they direct the church in maintaining sound doctrines; they equip the church for its work of proclamation. [F-2.01]

While Jesus Christ, as revealed in Scripture, is the most authoritative standard of our church, confessions are helpful in that they present the teachings of the Bible in relatively concise form. These subordinate standards give us interpretations of biblical doctrines as seen through the eyes of Christians from different times in history. The Barmen Declaration, for instance, was written by Christians facing subjugation by the Nazi movement in Germany.

Our *Book of Confessions* contains the following documents [see F-2.01–2.05]:

> The Nicene Creed
> The Apostles' Creed
> The Scots Confession
> The Heidelberg Catechism
> The Second Helvetic Confession
> The Westminster Confession of Faith
> The Larger and Shorter Catechisms
> The Theological Declaration of Barmen
> The Confession of 1967
> A Brief Statement of Faith—Presbyterian Church (U.S.A.)

While those in ordered ministries are not required to agree with everything in these confessions, they are required to

receive and adopt the essential tenets of the Reformed faith as expressed in the confessions of our church as authentic and reliable expositions of what Scripture leads us to believe and do and to be instructed and led by those confessions as they lead the people of God. [W-4.4003c]

Having a Constitution that includes creeds, confessions, and catechisms takes nothing away from the authority our church gives to the Scripture. Instead, these documents provide voices from the church's history that help us interpret the meaning of the Bible for our own day. They remind us that many Christians lived before us, and they call us to renew our commitment to the faith that is our heritage.

Whereas the *Book of Confessions* deals with what we believe, the *Book of Order* explains the workings of our church government. It seeks to collect and interpret biblical teachings about the church into a system of church government. Along with the Bible and the *Book of Confessions*, the *Book of Order* is one of the standards under which the church makes decisions and carries out its mission.

This part of our Constitution has four sections. They are the Foundations of Presbyterian Polity, the Form of Government, the Directory for Worship, and the Rules of Discipline. The basic principles and rules of our polity are outlined in the Foundations and the Form of Government. Among other things, these sections deal with the nature of the church, its confessions, and its mission. Also addressed are responsibilities of sessions and other councils, the way leaders are elected and ordained, the church's use of its property, the rules for meetings of congregations and councils, and our relationship to churches of other denominations.

The Directory for Worship contains our standards relating to worship (including funerals and weddings), the sacraments, admission to membership in the church, and the church's service in the world. The Rules of Discipline deals primarily with handling conflict and misconduct in the church.

To help readers with the task of interpreting our polity, in 1998 a portion of the Directory for Worship was moved to the Preface of the *Book of Order*. It states that:

In this *Book of Order*

1. "SHALL" and "IS TO BE/ARE TO BE" signify practice that is mandated,
2. "SHOULD" signifies practice that is strongly recommended,
3. "IS APPROPRIATE" signifies practice that is commended as suitable,
4. "MAY" signifies practice that is permissible but not required.

This information about interpreting language is helpful in understanding the relative authority of the material.

The need for a Constitution stems in part from the representative nature of our polity. Leaders are elected by the congregation to exercise authority on its behalf. A Constitution that details the precise boundaries of that authority keeps the leaders from assuming powers they were never intended to have. The *Book of Order* is essential equipment for all church leaders because it tells them not only the duties they must fulfill but also the powers they may exercise. Leaders are elected by the congregation to exercise authority on its behalf only as stated in the Constitution.

Relational. This characteristic of Presbyterian polity is rooted in our belief in the unity of the church. Ephesians 4:5–6 reminds us that all Christians have "one Lord, one faith, one baptism, one God and Father of us all." First Corinthians 12 compares the church to a human body with its many parts, stressing that we are indivisibly bound together in Christ. Another term for this one church is the "church universal."

The Presbyterian Church (U.S.A.), as a particular denomination of the church universal, tries to reflect this unity through participation in various national and international councils of churches. "It is our membership in the body of Christ that is the source of our ecumenical commitments" ("The Life and Mission Statement of the Presbyterian Church (U.S.A.)," 1985, par. 27.398). We also join with other denominations in doing the work of God whenever possible. We invite all those who have been baptized [W-2.4011a] to partake of the Lord's Supper with us. Our Constitution provides for recognizing the ordination of ministers from other denominations who are called to work in our churches [G-2.0505]. With the approval of the presbytery, Presbyterian congregations may join with congregations of other denominations in various forms of joint mision and witness [G-5.05]. In all these ways we seek to make visible the oneness of Christ's body.

Within itself, our denomination reflects the unity of the church universal through a common system of beliefs and a common polity. These twin ties of faith and government bind particular churches together into the Presbyterian Church (U.S.A.). Our common faith is expressed in Scripture as interpreted by our *Book of Confessions.* Our polity is expressed in the *Book of Order.*

The unity of the church is reflected in our polity in a number of ways. First, there are no independent Presbyterian churches. The very words are antithetical. To be Presbyterian is to be in relationship with other congregations and under the authority of a presbytery. A congregation can hold to Reformed theology while electing to be independent. However, it would hardly be justified in calling itself "Presbyterian," because that word itself implies the relational character of our polity. Presbyterian churches are by nature involved in the life and mission of the wider church.

The relational nature of our polity is also clearly reflected in its structure of councils. There are four of these: session, presbytery, synod, and the General Assembly [G-3.0101]. The session governs a particular congregation. A presbytery is composed of all the congregations and teaching elders within a certain geographical district. A synod functions in relation to three or more presbyteries. The General Assembly is the council of the whole denomination. It is one of the historic principles of our polity that the larger part of the Church, or a representation thereof, should govern the smaller [F-2.0203]. This means that more-inclusive councils have the power of review and control over less-inclusive ones.

Concerns and business also move upward from one council to another through the overture process. An overture is a request for consideration of a problem, for an action to be taken, or for a change to be made in some area of the church's life. Many changes to our *Book of Order* originate through the overture process. Presbyteries may send overtures to synod or to the General Assembly. Synods also may send overtures to the Assembly. Sessions may send overtures to presbytery about matters of interest to the wider church.

In matters of discipline, more-inclusive councils have jurisdiction over cases of judicial process brought to them from less-inclusive ones. These judicial responsibilities of councils are discussed in chapter 13 of this book.

A further implication of the church's unity is that many actions of councils are done on behalf of the denomination as a whole. When a presbytery examines a candidate for ordination, it is doing so for the whole church. When a session accepts a person into the membership of the congregation, it is acting for the church at large. Ruling elders are ordained, not just for their particular congregation, but for the denomination. It is this intimate relationship that makes effective means of review and control necessary.[3]

The Powers and Responsibilities of Councils

The *Book of Order* says several important things about the power of councils. First, any power that the church exercises rightfully comes from Jesus Christ. Christ alone is head of the church, and no human being or group should usurp his Lordship. The authority of councils is "only ministerial and declarative" [F-3.0107]. This means that the pronouncements and rules of councils should be based on the will of God revealed in Scripture. The councils do not have power to require things that the Scripture does not require. As the Westminster Confession of Faith says:

> God alone is Lord of the conscience, and hath left it free from the doctrines and commandments of men [sic] which are in anything contrary to his Word, or beside it in matters of faith or worship. (XXII, 2)

Second, the power of the church is strictly that of moral and spiritual influence [F-3.0108]. It is the power of loving concern, not of punishment.

There was a time when a person could be locked in the village stocks for religious offenses, but our polity clearly says that no civil penalties can be sought for religious wrongdoing.

Third, the particular powers of councils are only those stated in the Constitution. The session has no mandate to be a dictator in the congregation. It can exercise only the authority that has been given to it in the *Book of Order*. For example, sessions have the power to "determine occasions, days, times, and places for worship" [W-1.4004f], but they do not have the power to tell the minister what Scripture passages he or she shall read in the service. Presbyteries have the power to examine ministers for admission into the presbytery, but they do not have the power to refuse them admission purely on the basis of their race or sex. Each council has certain expressed powers, and only those powers, to exercise.

The principles outlined above help our churches to function in ways that are generally efficient, fair, and orderly.

The presbyterian system was formed out of a deep respect for the ability of church members to participate in their own government. It gives ultimate allegiance only to Jesus Christ. Its structures and polity are designed to further the mission of the church, to promote discipleship, and to build up the body of Christ.

Questions for Reflection and Discussion

1. What faith tradition did you grow up in? What do you remember about its church government?

2. How would you explain how the PC(USA) governs itself to a Baptist friend? An Episcopal friend?

3. How is Presbyterian polity similar to the U.S. system of government?

4. If someone asked you to explain the ways Presbyterian polity is founded on Scripture, how would you reply?

Chapter Two

CALLING
TO LEADERSHIP
IN THE CHURCH

Jane had been very active in Second Presbyterian Church. She had taught the junior high church school class, been a member of the choir, and served on the committee that visited newcomers to the community. When a member of the nominating committee asked if she was willing to serve as a ruling elder, Jane's amazed response was, "But I don't feel called!"

David's experience was different. While still a relatively new member of the Presbyterian Church (U.S.A.), he was asked to consider serving as a deacon. He agreed to do so without much thought. He viewed the prospect of being a church leader in a very matter-of-fact way. There was a job to be done, and he was willing to give it a try. After his election by the congregation, David began a series of study sessions with the other newly elected leaders. When the pastor, who led the leadership training classes, spoke of being called to office in the church, David was thoroughly confused.

Presbyterians have long emphasized the concept of God's call to church leadership, but not everyone is clear as to the meaning of the term "call." Some, like Jane, have focused on the "inner call," that special feeling that God does indeed have a special use for one's particular talents and abilities. Others have stressed the church's seeking out someone to fulfill a specific function—the call that comes as an unexpected "tap on the shoulder," to which the first response is often, "Who, me?" What do we mean when we speak of being called to church leadership?

The Calling to Church Membership

Calling to leadership must always be understood within the context of the calling to church membership. The beginning point is a faithful response to the good news of God's redemption of human life through the life, death, and resurrection of Jesus Christ. The sacrament of baptism is the sign of entry into membership in the Christian church. In baptism, believers, or the parents of a child receiving the sacrament, acknowledge faith in Jesus

Christ as Savior, trust in God's grace, and commit themselves to a life of discipleship. Calling to church membership is essentially the call of Christ, "Follow me."

Those who respond in faith, together with their children, claim their membership in the body of Christ through the sacrament of baptism. When a person makes a public profession of faith in Jesus Christ as Savior and Lord, that person accepts Christ's call to responsible involvement in the church's ministry and usually becomes an active member of a congregation.

The Presbyterian Church (U.S.A.) places substantial emphasis on the maning of church membership. A faithful member accepts Christ's call to be involved responsibly in the ministry of his Church. Such involvement includes:

a. proclaiming the good news in word and deed,
b. taking part in the common life and worship of a congregation,
c. lifting one another up in prayer, mutual concern, and active support,
d. studying Scripture and the issues of Christian faith and life,
e. supporting the ministry of the church through the giving of money, time, and talents,
f. demonstrating a new quality of life within and through the church,
g. responding to God's activity in the world through service to others,
h. living responsibly in the personal, family, vocational, political, cultural, and social relationships of life,
i. working in the world for peace, justice, freedom, and human fulfillment,
j. participating in the governing responsibilities of the church, and
k. reviewing and evaluating regularly the integrity of one's membership, and considering ways in which one's participation in the worship and service of the church may be increased and made more meaningful. [G-1.0304]

This listing includes both specific and general responsibilities. The more specific ones relate to the internal life of the church or to the life of the individual participating in the common life and worship of a congregation: praying; studying the Bible and the faith; giving of money, time, and talents in support of the work of the church; and participating in the governing responsibilities assigned to church members in the Form of Government.

The more general responsibilities relate both to life within the community of faith and to life beyond that community: proclaiming the good news; demonstrating a new quality of life; serving others in response to God's activity in the world; struggling for peace, justice, freedom, and human fulfillment within oneself, in the family, and around the world.

From the statements on the meaning of membership in the *Book of Order* it can be seen that membership in the church is no casual decision, no minor commitment. It is the testimony of the Presbyterian Church (U.S.A.) that when one responds to the call of Christ to discipleship and claims membership in the church, one is beginning a faith journey that affects all of life.

Church Membership as Ministry

Emphasis should be placed on the use of the term "ministry" in the section quoted above. All church members are called to ministry. Ministry is not limited to those functions performed by ordained persons. Ministry is the work of the whole church and every member of it. A study book issued by the General Assembly makes this point:

> From the moment that we transfer the responsibility for ministry to a selected or elected group, we have gone down a dead-end street. For although we may be deeply concerned to have an effective ministry, we will necessarily forget that we have been called, one and all, to be the ministry of Jesus Christ. We will be unable to understand the import of the simple statement which (perhaps more accurately than any other) describes the very being of the church: the church is the ministry of Jesus Christ.[1]

The reaching out of any Christian person to another human being is a work of ministry. The witness of a congregation that takes a stand on an issue of concern in the community in God's name is a work of ministry. This understanding of ministry is essential to the faithfulness and integrity of the church. The church has been damaged far too long by the attitude of "Let the pastor do it," perhaps even without the help of the other church leaders, much less the whole membership. How different it is when church members claim for themselves the full responsibilities of membership and of ministry!

The *Book of Order* also places accountability on persons for fulfilling their responsibilities of membership. Those who accept membership in the church make a binding commitment to Jesus Christ. That commitment is honored by "reviewing and evaluating regularly the integrity of one's membership, and considering ways in which one's participation in the worship and service of the church may be increased and made more meaningful" [G-1.0304]. Members are accountable to God and to the church for fulfilling the commitment of membership.

Calling to Leadership

The Presbyterian Church believes that certain responsibilities within the life of the church should be assigned to leaders who have been called and ordained to fulfill these particular functions. Any person considering accepting a call to church leadership should first review the responsibilities of church members and evaluate his or her own present involvement in the ministry of the body of Christ. Then that person can consider a call to perform specific leadership tasks.

How does the Presbyterian Church (U.S.A.) understand calling to church leadership? First, it is none other than the triune God who calls to leadership in the church. God in Christ through the Holy Spirit calls by giving gifts and abilities to certain members, which qualify them to perform special functions in the life of the Christian community.

How is this call known? The Reformed family of faith claims that God's call is known in three ways. One way is that the church seeks out those who give evidence of having the God-given gifts required for the job—such qualities as spiritual maturity, discernment, leadership ability, sensitivity to the needs of others, dependability, enthusiasm, theological awareness, and administrative skills. The congregation, through its members, takes the initiative to locate those persons within the church whom God may be calling into service as teaching elders, ruling elders, or deacons. The church then challenges them to share their gifts by responding positively to the request to serve. The congregation further indicates its desire to have certain persons as its leaders by actually electing them to leadership in a regularly called congregational meeting. The process of the election fulfills a fundamental principle of Presbyterian polity: namely, that no person is to be placed in any installed ministry in a congregation without being elected by that body [G-2.0102].

Another way in which Presbyterians recognize God's call is through the inner experience of the person involved. How does the person feel about the possible new work? Is there a willingness to become involved? Does the person feel, in some way, that this new opportunity is in accordance with God's will for her or his life? Is the timing right? The judgments of the person on these questions are significant. However, the Reformed tradition has often considered them less important than the church's judgment about the suitability of the person for the particular task.

The candidate for ordered ministry may feel like the person in the Gospel account who responded to Jesus, "I believe; help my unbelief!" (Mark 9:24).

Doubts about one's abilities and feelings of inadequacy for the task may well be very appropriate early responses to the call to ordered ministry in the church. Think of the biblical stories of God's call in which persons argue with God, convinced that God has made a mistake, that God intends to be calling someone with more skills or someone more worthy. A person may well prefer to dismiss all thought of accepting leadership in the church and yet find that the idea will not go away. God's call may involve a certain wrestling with unwelcome challenges. It is in times of such struggle that the church's view that the person is indeed fitted for ordered ministry may well become a decisive confirmation of God's call.

A final way in which God's call is made known is through the "concurring judgment of a council of the church" [G-2.0103]. In the case of those elected by the congregation to serve as ruling elders or deacons, the council is the church session, which has the responsibility of preparing and examining those elected to ordered ministry. The session must satisfy itself as to their personal faith; knowledge of doctrine, church government, and discipline as set forth in the Constitution; and understanding of the duties of the ministry [G-2.0402]. Only then is the service of ordination and installation conducted.

Qualifications and Gifts of Church Leaders

What qualifies one to be a church leader? The *Book of Order* states that the standard for all ordered ministries is the ministry of Jesus [G-2.0101], and thereby one of service. Given the daunting responsibilities of these ministries, it is easy for any prospective leader to think that he or she does not measure up. The persons that the nominating committee feels would make good leaders need to listen carefully to what the committee says about their gifts and prayerfully consider the request. The church, led by its leaders, moves forward in faith, trusting in God's grace to make us more than we are. God promises to give leaders the gifts they need to carry out their particular piece of this service.

There are particular qualifications mentioned for both ruling elders and deacons. A particular qualification for the ministry of ruling elder is that they should be "persons of wisdom and maturity of faith, having demonstrated skills in leadership and being compassionate in spirit" [G-2.0301]. Ruling elders must be equipped to help the congregation discern and follow God's will. Deacons should be people of "spiritual character, honest repute, exemplary lives, brotherly and sisterly love, sincere compassion, and sound judgment" [G-2.0201]. These characteristics fit the nature of their ordered ministry, which is one of taking the ministry of the church to anyone in distress.

Speaking of all those in ordered ministries, our Constitution [G-2.0104a] specifies:

In addition to possessing the necessary gifts and abilities, those who undertake particular ministries should be persons of strong faith, dedicated discipleship, and love of Jesus Christ as Savior and Lord. Their manner of life should be a demonstration of the Christian gospel in the church and in the world. They must have the approval of God's people and the concurring judgment of a council of the church.

Until 1997 the above-quoted section was all that the Form of Government said about the personal qualifications required of all church leaders. There were some additional particular characteristics needed for each of the three ordered ministries, but the qualities required in all leaders were summarized in very few words: All must be persons of "strong faith, dedicated discipleship, and love of Jesus Christ as Savior and Lord."

Ordination and Sexuality

In the late 1970s the landscape of ordination became increasingly complicated and fraught with conflict with regards to ordination of homosexual persons. Before the 1983 reunion of the UPCUSA and the PCUS, each church held its own General Assembly meeting annually. The position of the two churches was basically the same.

In 1976, an overture came to the UPCUSA General Assembly asking for guidance and clarification regarding the denomination's position on homosexuality. At the UPCUSA General Assembly in 1978, a paper was adopted declaring that homosexuality did not manifest God's plan for human sexuality. It also indicated that self-affirmed, sexually active homosexual persons were not eligible for ordination.

In 1977, the General Assembly of the PCUS adopted a study that affirmed the need for just treatment of homosexuals but declared that homosexuality falls short of God's plan. This action placed self-affirmed, sexually active homosexual persons outside candidacy for ordination.

After the reunion in 1983, the issues around the church's response to homosexuality began to take up a major share of the new denomination's attention. Year by year, the divisions around this issue grew deeper and more divisive. In addition to pronouncements of the General Assembly, some of the action around the issue of homosexuality and ordination was played out in the church's judicial arena.

Then in 1997, a new provision was added to the Form of Government's basic statement of qualification for all persons in ordered ministries. This new section spelled out explicitly the standard of sexual behavior required for ordination. In that version of the *Book of Order*, G-6.0106b stated:

Those who are called to office in the church are to lead a life in obedience to Scripture and in conformity to the historic standards of the church. Among these standards is the requirement to live either in fidelity within the covenant of marriage between a man and a woman (W-4.9001), or chastity in singleness. Persons refusing to repent of any self-acknowledged practice, which the confessions call sin, shall not be ordained and/or installed as deacons, elders, or ministers of the Word and Sacrament.

The 209th General Assembly (1997) that declared that G-6.0106b had been enacted also had before it many overtures that sought to change this provision of the Form of Government. Since then, the conflict over understandings of homosexuality and Scripture have continued to be played out in the arena of polity, especially around ordination. Almost every General Assembly from 1997 until the present has dealt with such matters. Many related cases of judicial process were also filed and brought to trial.

In recent years, the 217th General Assembly (2006) approved the report of the Task Force on the Peace, Unity, and Purity of the Church. This report proposed that candidates being examined for ordered ministry may declare a departure from the standards of the church on points of belief or practice. The body examining the candidate was then charged with determining whether that departure from the Scripture and Constitution of the church was serious enough to bar the candidate from being ordained or installed. This proposal was adopted by the Assembly. However before it could be fully tested, in 2008, the 218th General Assembly changed the landscape of ordination once again.

This Assembly voted to adopt an Authoritative Interpretation to the effect that "Interpretive statements concerning ordained service of homosexual church members by the 190th General Assembly of the United Presbyterian Church in the United States of America and the 119th General Assembly of the Presbyterian Church in the United States and all subsequent affirmations thereof, have no further force or effect."[2] This Assembly also sent a proposed constitutional change to the presbyteries that would remove G-6.0106b from the *Book of Order*. This proposed amendment did not receive the majority of presbytery votes.

In 2010, the 219th General Assembly voted to send to the presbyteries a proposed amendment to the Constitution removing G-6.0106b and replacing it with the following:

Standards for ordained service reflect the church's desire to submit joyfully to the Lordship of Jesus Christ in all aspects of life (F-1.02). The council responsible for ordination and/or installation (G-2.0402; G-2.0607; G-3.0306) shall examine each candidate's calling, gifts, preparation, and suitability for the responsibilities of ordered ministry. The examination shall include, but not be limited to, a determination of the candidate's ability and commitment to fulfill all the requirements as expressed in the constitutional questions for

ordination and installation (W-4.4003). Councils shall be guided by
Scripture and the confessions in applying standards to individual
candidates.

This amendment was approved by 97 of 173 presbyteries and was enacted
on July 10, 2011. It is now found in the Form of Government in G-2.0104b.

The effect of this section of the Form of Government is to lift the
prohibition against ordaining persons who engage in sexual behavior
outside the context of marriage between a man and a woman. Ordaining
bodies may inquire about the sexual behavior of candidates and take
the information received into consideration in making their decisions.
The absolute bar, however, against ordaining persons who engage in
sexual behavior outside marriage between a man and a woman has been
removed. Significant difference of opinion remains in the denomination
on this issue. How this will play itself out in our polity over the coming
years remains to be seen.[3]

Ordination to Ordered Ministries

Ordination is the act by which the church admits persons to leadership,
placing them within the "ordering" of the church's life. Those ordained as
ruling and teaching elders and as deacons are not *separated out* from the
people of God but rather *placed into* special tasks within the people of God.
In the words of the *Book of Order*:

> "The existence of these ordered ministries in no way diminishes the
> importance of the commitment of all members to the total ministry
> of the church." [G-2.0102]

It is important to consider the constitutional questions that must be
answered in the affirmative by those being ordained to leadership. Many
of the questions asked of teaching elders, ruling elders, and deacons are
identical. All those assuming any ordered ministry in the Presbyterian
Church (U.S.A.) make certain basic commitments as to their faith in Jesus
Christ as Lord of all and Head of the Church and in the triune God, their
acceptance of the Scripture as God's Word, and their adoption of the essential beliefs of the Reformed faith as expressed in the *Book of Confessions*.
All promise to be instructed and led by the confessions in their leadership
of the church, to be governed by the polity of the Presbyterian Church
(U.S.A.), to abide by its discipline, and to work collegially in ministry. All
promise to lead lives that seek to follow Christ, to love neighbors, and to
work for the reconciliation of the world. All promise also to further the
peace, unity, and purity of the church and to seek to serve God's people
with energy, intelligence, imagination, and love.

All those in ordered ministry are asked if they will fulfill their respective ministries in obedience to Jesus Christ, under the authority of Scripture, and if they will be continually guided by the confessions. Each person being ordained as a ruling elder is then asked, "Will you be a faithful ruling elder, watching over the people, providing for their worship, nurture, and service? Will you share in government and discipline, serving in councils of the church, and in your ministry will you try to show the love and justice of Jesus Christ?" [W-4.4003i(1)].

Deacons are asked the following: "Will you be a faithful deacon, teaching charity, urging concern, and directing the people's help to the friendless and those in need? In your ministry will you try to show the love and justice of Jesus Christ?" [W-4.4003i(2)].

The congregation is then asked to affirm the election of these new leaders by agreeing to accept them, to encourage them, to respect their decisions, and to follow their guidance, in all these things serving Jesus Christ, the Head of the Church [W-4.4004a].

By answering the constitutional questions affirmatively, the newly ordained leader becomes more accountable to the Presbyterian Church (U.S.A.). The leader binds himself or herself more closely to the faith and polity of the church. At ordination the leader affirms that the faith of the Reformed confessions is indeed one's own faith and that she or he will be led by the faith of the Reformed family in providing leadership to the church. The leader's commitment to Presbyterian polity and discipline is a more explicit one than that assumed by unordained active church members. An active member is defined as one who "has voluntarily submitted to the government of this church" [G-1.0402].

An ordained leader promises to be "governed by our church's polity" and to "abide by its discipline" [W-4.4003e]. The person also promises to live and work in such a way as to promote the peace, unity, and purity of the church. Implicit in this commitment is the agreement, as far as conscience permits, to abide by the decisions of the session, board of deacons, presbytery, synod, or General Assembly even when one disagrees with the decision or has actively supported another point of view. All actions of ordained leaders are carried out in conformity to the church's constitution.

In the Presbyterian understanding, ordination itself confers no special gifts but rather recognizes those gifts already given by God in calling a person to leadership. There is no magic, no sudden difference in a person following ordination. Abilities are recognized, God's calling acknowledged, and prayers offered for God's blessing upon those ordained as they assume new responsibilities and undertake new tasks. In ordination, some members of the body are being "set into" a disciplined and purposeful activity in the life of the church.[4] The purpose of ordination is to enable Christ's body, the church, to work together as a whole, in order that the ministry and mission of the church might be fulfilled.

The Presbyterian Church (U.S.A.) understands ordered ministry as being perpetual. Ruling elders and deacons may be elected for limited terms of active service, but they still hold their ordained status when their active service ends. If reelected to active service in the same ministry role they are not reordained. Even if not in active service, ruling elders and deacons can still serve the church in certain functions of office. Within the particular church, any ordained leader may serve the Lord's Supper to the people. (This privilege may be extended to any member upon the invitation of the session [W-3.3616d].)

The Reformed understanding of how the church is ordered and of the functions fulfilled by its ordained leaders has been worked out over many centuries, in many countries, and in a great variety of situations. A look at the history of the Reformed church shows much growth, change, and adaptability in the Presbyterian system. From the time of John Calvin, Reformed Christians have emphasized the principle that persons other than ministers are to serve as church leaders. Calvin envisioned four ministries: pastor or minister, elder, deacon, and doctor. The doctor, in Calvin's concept, was a learned teacher who preserved and passed on knowledge but did not assume the responsibilities of preaching and administering the sacraments. (By the middle of the seventeenth century, the doctoral ministry was assimilated into that of pastor or minister.)[5] Calvin saw elders as those who, along with pastors, made the decisions of governance. Deacons exercised ministries of compassion. Calvin did not emphasize the ordination of leaders other than ministers. That emphasis was to come later.

Freedom of Conscience and Its Limitations

It has been emphasized that ordination to church leadership makes persons more accountable to the church. This accountability includes accepting some limitations on the leader's freedom of conscience. The key passage is G-2.0105:

> It is necessary to the integrity and health of the church that the persons who serve in it in ordered ministries shall adhere to the essentials of the Reformed faith and polity as expressed in this Constitution. So far as may be possible without serious departure from these standards, without infringing on the rights and views of others, and without obstructing the constitutional governance of the church, freedom of conscience with respect to the interpretation of Scripture is to be maintained. It is to be recognized, however, that in entering the ordered ministries of the Presbyterian Church (U.S.A.) one chooses to exercise freedom of conscience within certain bounds. His or her conscience is captive to the Word of God

as interpreted in the standards of the church so long as he or she continues to seek, or serve in, ordered ministry. The decision as to whether a person has departed from essentials of Reformed faith and polity is made initially by the individual concerned but ultimately becomes the responsibility of the council in which he or she is a member.

Freedom of conscience in the interpretation of Scripture is recognized insofar as the exercise of freedom of conscience does not lead to serious departure from the essentials of the Reformed faith and polity as expressed in the church's Constitution, does not infringe on the rights and views of others, and does not obstruct the constitutional governance of the church. Freedom of conscience may not be used by a person in ordered ministry as a reason for holding beliefs contrary to the essentials of the *Book of Confessions*, infringing on the rights of other church members, or refusing to act in accordance with the *Book of Order*. If leaders find themselves unable to abide by the doctrine or polity of the church without violating their consciences, they should counsel with God and fellow believers as to the most faithful course of action.

The Presbyterian Church (U.S.A.) affirms that God calls the church's leaders by giving them the gifts necessary for fulfilling the task. This call is known through the church's seeking out of the person, the feeling of willingness on the part of the person, and the concurrence of the appropriate council. The church ordains those who have been called, acknowledging by that ordination the new responsibilities being assumed and the seriousness of the task. By affirming the constitutional questions of ordination, the leader places himself or herself in a position of greater accountability to the church. Through this whole process, the church "orders" its common life to enable the ministry of the whole people of God.

Questions for Reflection and Discussion

1. How do you feel about being called to be an ordained leader in the church?

2. Think of ruling elders or deacons you have known who fulfilled their calling well. What made them so good at their service as a leader?

3. If there is one thing you would like to accomplish in your service as an ordained leader, what would it be?

4. How have you experienced the denomination or your local

congregation dealing with homosexual persons, especially those called to serve as leaders?

5. What do the words, "demonstrating a new quality of life within and through the church" [G-1.0304] mean to you? Describe a person you know who has fulfilled this responsibility of membership in the church.

Chapter Three

ELECTION
OF
CHURCH LEADERS

The nominating committee of Tall Pines Presbyterian Church was bogged down in a major debate between two members over the proper procedure for electing ruling elders. The committee planned to nominate two persons for every vacancy and anticipated additional nominations from the floor. One committee member wanted to expedite the election by asking that the three persons receiving the highest number of votes be declared elected. Another member said that she thought the *Book of Order* requires each nominee to receive a majority of the votes cast to be elected.

The Frontier Presbyterian Church found itself without a pastor after twelve years of a very meaningful pastoral relationship. A pastor nominating committee was elected in accordance with the *Book of Order*. At their first meeting the members of the committee looked at one another and one voiced what most were feeling: "How do we know where to begin? Finding the right pastor for our church seems like an impossible task!"

A basic principle of Presbyterian polity is the right of every congregation to elect its own installed leaders. This right is exercised when the congregation chooses some from among its members to serve as ruling elders and deacons. It is also exercised when the congregation, with the approval of presbytery, calls a pastor, co-pastor, or associate pastor. The purpose of this chapter is to explain the process of electing leaders and also to talk about some of the important principles involved.

The Nominating Committee

The process of electing ruling elders and deacons in the local congregation begins with a nominating committee. This committee is made up of members of the congregation and is elected by the congregation. The Form of Government gives a fair amount of freedom to congregations in creating this important committee. It requires, however, that the committee be made up of at least three active members of the congregation. This number must include at least one active session member. The pastor is also a member of the committee by virture of position and can participate fully in the committee's business with the exception of voting.

So that the whole congregation shall be represented in the nominating process, the Form of Government instructs that the makeup of the committee shall reflect the church's membership. Conditions to be taken into account here include race, ethnicity, age, sex, disability, geography, and theological conviction [F-1.0403]. A representative nominating committee helps make sure that the slate of leaders that the congregation will have to vote on when the election comes is inclusive of the church's membership. Another provision that helps that to happen is the requirement that, at the election, nominations from the floor will always be called for [G-2.0401]. Any active member of the congregation is eligible for consideration.

Each congregational nominating committee is free to decide how to do its work. Practices vary from congregation to congregation. Some committees nominate one person for every vacancy; others nominate one or two more persons than they have vacancies; still others nominate two or more times as many persons as vacancies. Some congregations rarely, if ever, have nominations from the floor, thus increasing the importance of the committee's work. One thing is clear, however: the opportunity for nominations from the floor *must always* be provided.

Election, Preparation, and Examination
of Ruling Elders and Deacons

It is a wise practice, but not required, for the nominating committee to make sure that a person they intend to nominate is willing to serve before putting the name before the congregation. In the case of nominations from the floor, the former Form of Government required that those nominated must have given permission for their names to be put forward and must agree to serve if elected. Our present Form of Government does not include this provision. Therefore, any eligible nomination from the floor must be included on the ballot. This is true even though that member might later decline to serve and thus make it necessary for the congregation to reconvene for the purpose of electing another ruling elder or deacon.

The actual election of members of a church's session and board of deacons takes place at a duly-called meeting of the congregation. The provisions for this meeting are the same as for any congregational meeting. It is appropriate for the moderator to explain the process of nomination and to introduce and thank the members of the nominating committee for their work. After giving those present and eligible to vote the opportunity to make a nomination, the congregation votes. Each congregation may decide how to take the vote. In order to be elected, a nominee must receive a majority of all the votes cast.

It is the duty of the session to provide a period of study and preparation for the newly elected leaders before they begin their work [G-2.0402]. Neglecting leadership training is a great disservice not only to the new ruling elders and deacons but to the whole congregation as well. Just answering the constitutional questions with integrity requires a certain level of knowledge many people may not have. Disregarding training devalues the significance of ruling elders and deacons in the congregation's life. Pastors should work with the session to make sure that new leaders are given everything they need to serve well.

The nature and extent of this leadership training will vary somewhat depending on how many new leaders are being ordained. Returning leaders should be strongly encouraged to attend training again since some things will have changed since they last served. It is the responsibility of the session to make sure that each person newly elected to ordered ministry has essential knowledge of the "doctrine, government, and discipline contained in the Constitution of the church" [G-2.0402].

Along with these topics, new leaders should be trained in basic church history, the history and traditions of their own congregation, ways in which to handle conflict, the mission of the church, the skills of spiritual leadership, and the duties of ruling elders and deacons. A minimum of twelve hours instruction should be offered.

After the training period, the session is required to examine the new leaders. The form this examination takes is left up to each session to decide. However, it should take seriously the investment the candidates have made in their training. If leadership training has been taken seriously, the examination can be a time for leaders to share what they have learned and what it means to them.

Part of the examination will include a time for new leaders to share what their Christian faith means to them personally. Every ruling elder and deacon should be able to give a brief, authentic witness about their experience of God and the difference it makes in his or her life. It is helpful to take time in the training period to help leaders reflect on these things and help them learn to talk about them gracefully. In preparing to talk about their personal faith with the session, many people find it helpful to write a brief statement of what they believe and what their faith means in their life. Hearing new leaders give their Christian witness is one of the most inspiring things that sessions can do together.

After the examination of newly elected leaders has been approved and they have confirmed their willingness to serve, the session shall determine when the service of ordination and installation is to be held. "The service of ordination and installation shall focus upon Christ and the joy and responsibility of serving him through the mission and ministry of the church, and shall include a sermon appropriate to the occasion" [G-2.0403]. The required order for this service is given in the Directory for

Worship [W-4.4000]. The constitutional questions asked of ruling elders and deacons and of the congregation of which they shall be leaders are discussed in the preceding chapter of this book. It may be of value to review that discussion.

Calling a Pastor

In addition to electing ruling elders and deacons to serve in leadership positions, Presbyterian congregations also elect teaching elders (also called ministers of the Word and Sacrament and pastors) to serve in pastoral relationships. When a congregation elects (and thereby calls) a teaching elder to serve in an unlimited or permanent pastoral relationship, that minister is installed by the presbytery to serve as pastor, co-pastor, or associate pastor of the congregation. Chapter 7 of this book discusses in detail the various types of pastoral relationships and the differences among them. Here it is important to understand the process for calling pastors by congregations and to see that process within the context of the election of all church leaders.

Let us assume that the church has consulted with the presbytery and received its permission for the church to seek a pastor. (The procedure about to be described would be the same if the congregation were seeking co-pastors or an associate pastor.) The next step is for the session to call a congregational meeting for the purpose of electing a pastor nominating committee (PNC). The congregation shall be given adequate public notice of the time, place, and purpose of the meeting [G-1.0502]. The only specification about the makeup of the nominating committee is that it be "representative of the whole congregation." Once again the church's principle of inclusiveness in diversity is emphasized. How the nominating committee itself is to be nominated is not covered in the Form of Government. The session may suggest the makeup of the committee and may even make nominations for the committee, or it may appoint a committee to nominate the PNC. Of course, nominations must be permitted from the floor for any committee elected by the congregation.

At its congregational meeting the congregation may amend the session's proposal on any of the matters concerning the pastor nominating committee: its size, makeup, method of being selected, and the particular church members to serve on the committee. Because of the extreme importance of the work of the PNC, it is certainly in the interest of the congregation to make all decisions concerning it with care.

The Form of Government gives almost complete freedom to pastor nominating committees in how they go about their task. This was also true of the former Form of Government. Two sentences come between the election of the committee and the committee's readiness to bring a potential pastor's name before the congregation:

> According to the process of the presbytery and prior to making its report to the congregation, the pastor nominating committee shall receive and consider the presbytery's counsel on the merits, suitability, and availability of those considered for the call. When the way is clear for the committee to report to the congregation, the committee shall notify the session, which shall call a congregational meeting. [G-2.0803]

Conferring with presbytery advisers will also provide access to a wide variety of helps. Many presbyteries appoint a liaison to work intentionally and personally with each PNC. This liaison can introduce the PNC to a large number of resources that have been produced by other presbyteries and by the denomination. He or she can also help the committee learn to work with the denomination's Church Leadership Connection in developing a church information form that is used in the matching process. In this process a computer locates ministers or candidates for the ministry who have talents and interests similar to those requested by the particular church. It should be noted that a PNC is required to confer with the presbytery before making its recommendation to the congregation. The mandatory word "shall" is used in the section of the Form of Government quoted above.

In keeping with the principles of inclusiveness stated in F-1.0403 the PNC's search should not be limited to persons of a particular racial ethnic background, sex, marital status, or age. Candidates with disabilities should also be considered. In other words, the committee should be open to finding a minister who, while having all the qualifications to serve, may bring new perspectives and new insights to the church's ministry.

When the PNC has located the person it hopes to nominate as pastor, it must work very closely with the presbytery and with the church's session in composing the terms of call and in seeing that all steps of the calling process are properly completed. The PNC should be very careful not to make commitments to the candidate that the session is not willing to stand behind. Therefore, the timing of various steps in the process becomes extremely important. The Form of Government requires that "The terms of call shall always meet or exceed any minimum requirement of the presbytery in effect when the call is made" [G-2.0804].

Presbyteries Working Together

As the PNC completes its work, it often has a good opportunity to learn firsthand about the interdependence of presbyteries. If the minister or candidate for ministry whom the committee desires to call is under the jurisdiction of a different presbytery from the one of which the church is part, then the two presbyteries must work together in fulfilling their responsibilities.

In the case of a minister, the presbytery of which the minister has been a member must dismiss the minister to the presbytery in which the new church is located (the presbytery of call). If that minister has been serving as a pastor, they must dissolve the pastoral relationship between the minister and the church in which the minister has been serving. The presbytery of call must examine the minister for membership in that new presbytery, seeking information as to the minister's "Christian faith and views in theology, the Sacraments, and the government of this church" [G-3.0306]. The presbytery should also make sure that the pastor's terms of call meet its standards before the call is executed.

In the case of a candidate, the presbytery that has supervised the candidate during the time of preparation for ministry must approve the candidate who is beginning to negotiate a call to serve. This approval involves a process of certifying that the candidate has met all the requirements listed in G-2.0607a-d. When the presbytery of preparation is fully satisfied as to the candidate's readiness to be examined for ordination as a teaching elder, it certifies the candidate as "ready for examination for ordination, pending a call" [G-2.0607]. A written record shall be kept of when this certification occurs. Then it is usually the calling presbytery that examines, ordains and installs the new teaching elder [G-2.0702]. The use of the word "ordinarily" instead of "shall" in this section gives some flexibility in this matter for candidates and presbyteries.

The provision that a presbytery must examine ministers and candidates seeking membership in the presbytery is an expression of another constitutional principle, namely, that a presbytery has the right to determine its own membership. A congregation may not call a particular person to be its pastor, co-pastor, or associate pastor unless the presbytery accepts that person into membership. If the presbytery declines to receive the minister (or candidate), then the PNC must seek another person to nominate to the congregation and once again seek presbytery approval.

Presbyteries may delegate some of their authority relating to the calling and examining of ministers and candidates for ministry to groups designated by the presbytery. When this happens, then that group actually acts on behalf of the entire presbytery. The group acting in this way must report its actions to the next stated meeting of the presbytery [G-3.0307].

The Form of Government gives no specific instructions for the congregational meeting to elect a pastor. It is assumed that the provisions for congregational meeting in G-1.0503 apply. When both presbytery and the congregation have approved the call and the candidate has accepted, the way is clear for installation, and ordination if necessary.

The ordination and installation of teaching elders parallels that of ruling elders and deacons. The Directory for Worship gives one set of instructions for all services of ordination and installation. [W-4.4000] "The service of ordination and installation shall focus upon Christ and the joy and responsibility of serving him through the mission and ministry of the church, and shall include a sermon appropriate to the occasion" [G-2.0403]. Eight of the nine constitutional questions used in these services for ruling elders, teaching elders, and deacons are identical. It is extremely significant that all three kinds of leaders make almost exactly the same commitment in terms of belief and quality of service. Each ministry is important, and each ordained leader has special functions in the congregation. They all work together so that the church may be effective in its life and mission and that God might be glorified.

Questions for Reflection and Discussion

1. How does your congregation nominate candidates for ruling elder and deacon to the congregation? How is the voting usually handled? What are the good and not-so-good things about this procedure?

2. What are the positives and negatives of nominating more than one person per leadership position to be filled?

3. How is the congregation invited to participate in the nominating process before the congregational meeting? If it is not, why not?

4. If you have served as an ordained leader before, what kind of training did you have? Was it helpful or not?

Chapter Four

THE ORDERED MINISTRY
OF
RULING ELDER

The newly elected ruling elders of Calvin Presbyterian Church were on a weekend retreat led by their teaching elder and a professor of polity from a Presbyterian seminary. The purpose of the retreat was to study those subjects in which newly elected leaders must be examined before they are ordained and installed. The teaching elder encouraged all participants to share their stories of experiencing God and growing in faith and led a discussion of Presbyterian doctrine. The professor dealt with government, discipline, and the duties of the ministry of ruling elder. One participant pointed out that Calvin Church would probably be run more efficiently if the congregation would authorize the teaching elder to make most decisions in the government of the church. The session would have to meet only rarely, if indeed the church needed a session at all! The seminary professor realized that these newly elected ruling elders needed an overview of the ministry of ruling elder and its importance for Presbyterians. She chose to begin with a look into the history of that ministry.

Early Reformers

The Reformed emphasis on the ordered ministry of ruling elder can be traced to several early Reformers, including John Calvin. When Calvin developed a polity for the governance of the church, he placed particular emphasis on the leaders of the church. An early emphasis of the Protestant Reformation had been on discarding practices of the Roman Catholic Church that the Reformers felt to be opposed to the teachings of Scripture. With regard to governance, Protestant Christians first decided how the church was *not* to be governed. Then they undertook the positive task of designing a system of governance, seeking to follow biblical principles as they built. John Calvin was faced with the particular task of developing a church organization for the city of Geneva. Studying the New Testament, Calvin identified ordered ministries that he considered to be permanent, that is, intended for the church in all times. One of these was the ordered ministry of "government," that is, the ordered ministry of ruling elder. Calvin concluded that the New Testament envisions two kinds of presbyters. Some presbyters have the responsibilities of preaching and teaching the Word. The other type of presbyter does not have this responsibility for proclamation, but along with the teaching elder shares the responsibility for governance within the church. Calvin placed particular emphasis on the discipline of personal conduct. Governance was almost synonymous with the correction of moral error or faults. Ruling elders were charged with oversight of the daily behavior of the people. Calvin organized the teaching elders and twelve ruling elders of the city of Geneva into one consistory—the forerunner of what we now know as a session. The consistory had responsibility for discipline. Its major concerns were that the people act according to the highest moral standards, that they participate regularly in worship, and that they become more knowledgeable of the Christian faith.

The influence of Calvin and the church at Geneva rapidly spread throughout Europe and Great Britain. Calvin encouraged his followers to adapt the system of church government begun in Geneva to their own particular situation.[1] Many variations on Calvin's system were developed. Churches throughout Europe developed written constitutions that systematized their ecclesiastical institutions. These constitutions were probably freely shared among the Reformed family. As Reformed leaders in one country attempted to solve their own problems of ecclesiastical organization, they kept a watchful eye on the solutions to similar problems advanced by reformers in other countries.[2]

The Church in Scotland

Because of the influence of Scotland on American Presbyterianism, it is important to pay particular attention to developments in polity in that country. The first Constitution of the Scottish Reformed Church was completed in 1560. The ministry of ruling elder was fairly well developed in this *First Book of Discipline*. Ruling elders were elected by the congregation after nomination by the retiring ruling elders and deacons, with members of the congregation eligible to make further nominations. Twice the number of persons to be elected were nominated by the retiring leaders, an indication that the congregation exercised a significant element of choice.

Ruling elders and deacons, as well as teaching elders, were subject to strict discipline by the Scottish church. The church in Scotland differed from Calvin's church in Geneva with regard to the role of deacons. In Scotland, deacons as well as ruling elders participated in governing responsibilities. The congregational court was called the consistory and was composed of ruling elders, teaching elders, and deacons. Of more importance than their difference over the rightful responsibilities of deacons was the agreement between the church in Geneva and that of Scotland that leaders other than teaching elders should be members of the group governing the church. The point of agreement was the participation of the ruling elder. Besides the role of deacons, the consistory of the Scottish church differed from that of Geneva in another important way. In Scotland each congregation had its own consistory, since the Scottish church covered a much larger area than the city of Geneva.

The Scottish consistory had three major areas of responsibility. The consistory administered ecclesiastical discipline, managed the general affairs of the congregation, and took a leading part in the election of the teaching elders of the congregation. (In exercise of this final responsibility, the deacons were excluded from the consistory.)[3] It is interesting to note that the Scottish consistory exercised discipline over all church leaders, including ministers, as well as over members of the congregation. In this respect the church in Scotland was more democratic than that in Geneva, which made a distinction between its discipline of office bearers and church members. Only teaching elders disciplined other teaching elders in the Genevan church.[4]

The *First Book of Discipline* attempted to serve an entire nation, but it soon became inadequate for its task. A revised constitution was drawn up between 1574 and 1578. This *Second Book of Discipline* introduced the council of the presbytery to meet the needs of a larger geographical area. The presbytery was to become the major contribution of Scotland to Presbyterian polity. The ordered ministry of ruling elder took on additional responsibilities with the introduction of presbyteries. The presbytery was composed of pastors, doctors, and ruling elders representing each kirk session within the district of the presbytery. (Doctors, or teachers, were the fourth church-ordered ministry in Calvin's polity, and these were carried over into the polity of the Church of Scotland for a period of time. Deacons lost their responsibilities for governance under the *Second Book of Discipline* and thus were not members of presbytery.) Although ruling elders were members of presbytery and urged to attend its meetings, they were not as obligated to participate as were the pastors and doctors. The pastors and doctors apparently summoned the ruling elders to attend particular meetings that dealt with important business. In fact, it was declared in 1582 that when the presbytery was exercising ecclesiastical discipline, the pastors and doctors must outnumber the ruling elders.[5]

The duties of presbytery were many and varied: making certain that the preaching within the churches of its district was orthodox, seeing that the sacraments were rightly administered, overseeing financial affairs, maintaining ecclesiastical discipline, and seeing that the actions of the Provincial and General Assemblies were carried out. Presbyteries could also enact rules to maintain order in their congregations, as long as the presbytery notified its Provincial Assembly. Again, what is most significant to note is that the presbytery, when it conducted its most important business, was not made up of pastors and doctors alone but included the participation of ruling elder representatives of the churches. It is also of interest to note that the council of the congregation, previously called the consistory, was called the "Kirk Eldership" or the "Session" in the *Second Book of Discipline*. According to the new constitution, ruling elders were ordained to active ministry for life. Previously they had been elected annually.[6]

Early Presbyterianism in America

When Presbyterians came to America, they brought with them their basic understanding of the ministry of ruling elder. There is evidence from as early as 1617 of at least one attempt to set up in the Colony of Virginia a church government with ruling elders and teaching elders. Four ruling elders were selected from among the membership of a parish.[7] One congregation in Maryland, after the death of its pastor in 1679, was led by a ruling elder until the new minister arrived, probably several years later.[8]

The first presbytery in America was founded in 1706 under the leadership of Francis Makemie. The first meeting of the presbytery was attended by teaching elders only. Ruling elders joined in subsequent meetings, however.[9] This Presbytery of Philadelphia included congregations from Maryland and Delaware as well as from the Philadelphia area. Later, churches from New Jersey and Long Island joined the presbytery. Growth was so fast that a synod of four presbyteries was organized in 1717. In these early years of organized Presbyterianism in America, the teaching elders exercised the major leadership. However, the ministry of ruling elder was clearly a part of American Presbyterian life from earliest days.

The synod, which became known as the Synod of New York and Philadelphia, determined in 1785 that a General Assembly consisting of elected delegates would be a more effective form of national organization than the existing synod, which was made up of all the teaching elders of the church and one ruling elder from every congregation. The synod meeting in 1788 adopted a constitution, including a Form of Government. It also organized a General Assembly with four constituent synods: New York and New Jersey, Philadelphia, Virginia, and the Carolinas. The first meeting of the General Assembly was called for in May 1789.

The 1788 Form of Government

The Constitution adopted by the synod of 1788 became the Constitution of the new General Assembly. It is to this Constitution that we must look to find the foundational statements on the ministry of ruling elder. This

Constitution contains a brief chapter, titled "Of Ruling Elders," which remained unchanged for nearly one hundred years. It reads as follows:

> Ruling elders are properly the representatives of the people, chosen by them for the purpose of exercising government and discipline, in conjunction with pastors or ministers. This office has been understood, by a great part of the Protestant Reformed Churches, to be designated in the holy Scriptures, by the title of governments; and of those who rule well, but do not labour in the word and doctrine. [IV]

Scriptural references accompany this chapter. First Timothy 5:17 and 1 Corinthians 12:18 are quoted in the notes. Two additional passages are cited: Romans 12:7–8 and Acts 15:25.

Another chapter of this Form of Government is titled "Of Electing and Ordaining Ruling Elders and Deacons." This chapter begins by stating that it is prescribing "the mode in which ecclesiastical rulers shall be ordained to their respective offices" [XII.1]. It is important to notice that the title of the chapter and the first section used the word "ordain." That word is not used, however, later in the chapter where the introduction into office is actually described. The chapter states that ruling elders are to be elected by the congregation "in the mode most approved and in use in that congregation" [XII.2]. Persons who are elected and indicate a willingness to accept the office take up their office during a service of worship. Following the preaching of the sermon, the newly elected ruling elders answer constitutional questions in the presence of the congregation. The ruling elders are then "set apart . . . by prayer" [XIII.4]. "An exhortation suited to the occasion" is to be given to the new ruling elders and to the congregation [XII.4].

The 1788 Form of Government states clearly the membership of each judicatory and the requirements for a quorum. "The Church session consists of the pastor or pastors, and ruling elders, of a particular congregation" [VIII.1]. The presbytery is made up of all the teaching elders within the presbytery and one ruling elder from each congregation. It is interesting to note the quorum of a presbytery:

> Any three ministers, and as many elders as may be present belonging to the presbytery, being met, at the time and place appointed, shall be a judicatory, competent to dispatch of business, not withstanding the absence of other members. [IX.4]

Apparently it was not necessary for *any* ruling elders to be present in order for the presbytery to meet. The synod is defined as a "convention of several presbyteries, within a larger district" [X.1]. The makeup of the General Assembly is defined as follows:

The General Assembly shall consist of an equal delegation of bishops [teaching elders] and elders [ruling elders] from each presbytery in the following proportions: viz. each presbytery consisting of not more than six ministers shall send one minister and one elder, each presbytery, consisting of more than six ministers and not more than twelve, shall send two ministers and two elders. [XI.2]

The listing continues, with the number of representatives increasing as the number of teaching elders increased, but in every case a presbytery sends the same number of ruling elders and teaching elders. It is interesting to note that for a quorum to be present at the General Assembly at least half of the quorum had to be made up of teaching elders. The Constitution does not say that half must be ruling elders. Apparently the quorum could be composed entirely of teaching elders [XI.3]. The sections concerning representation and the quorum in various judicatories are significant because of the struggles that occurred over the next century concerning the question of parity between ruling elders and teaching elders.

Advocacy for the Ordered Ministry of Ruling Elder

One of the early influential advocates for elevating the ministry of ruling elder to its proper dignity and responsibility was Dr. Samuel Miller of Princeton Theological Seminary. In 1832 Miller published a book titled *An Essay on the Warrant, Nature, and Duties of the Office of the Ruling Elder*. This book contains Miller's thinking on the subject of the ruling elder developed over a twenty-year period. In the introduction, in which the author states that his purpose is not to cause controversy but rather to benefit the church, Miller, referring to the ministry of ruling elder, states that some details of his opinions have changed over the years. However, he affirms "In reference to the Divine warrant and the great importance of the office for which I plead, my convictions have become stronger than ever."[10] As had been the custom of the Reformed tradition since its beginnings in the sixteenth century, Miller went into great detail to show the roots of the role of ruling elder in both Old and New Testaments and throughout church history. After six chapters of evidence, Miller concluded that ruling elders are absolutely necessary in the church.[11] One advantage to having a group of ruling elders exercising authority in a congregation is to protect the teaching elder from succumbing to the temptation of assuming too much power and authority. Also, a church with a group of responsible ruling elders can receive "all the principal advantages which might be expected to result from being under the pastoral care of four or five ministers," without having the disadvantage of having to support so many teaching elders.[12]

Miller distinguished between the corporate duties of the body of ruling elders and those duties that fall on the ruling elder as an individual. In considering the corporate responsibilities he made a strong case for the equality of the ruling elder with the pastor:

> In the Church Session, whether the Pastor be present or presiding or not, every member has an equal voice. The vote of the most humble and retiring Ruling Elder is of the same avail as that of his Minister. So that no Pastor can carry any measure unless he can obtain the concurrence of a majority of the Eldership. And as the whole spiritual government of each Church is committed to its bench of Elders, the Session is competent to regulate every concern, and to correct every-thing which they consider as amiss in the arrangements or affairs of the Church which admits of correction. Every individual of the Session, is of course, competent to propose any new service, plan, or measure, which he believes will be for the benefit of the congrega-tion, and if a majority of the Elders concur with him in opinion, it may be adopted.[13]

Because of his view of the nature and importance of the office, Miller questioned the practice of calling ruling elders "lay elders." To speak of teaching elders as clergy and ruling elders as part of the laity makes a distinction between these two classes of elders that is "out to convey an idea altogether erroneous, if not seriously mischievous."[14] He went back through early church history to show that the terms "clergy" and "clerical" were, in the early centuries of the church's history, applied to all classes of church leaders. Speaking of ruling elders, Miller reasoned:

> They are as really in office; they as really bear an office of Divine appointment, an office of a high and spiritual nature, and an office, the functions of which cannot be rightfully performed, but by those who are regularly set apart to it, as any other officer of the Christian Church. They are as really a portion of God's lot; as really set over the laity, or body of the people as the most distinguished and venerated minister of Jesus can be. Whether, therefore, we refer to early usage, or to strict philological import, Ruling Elders are truly entitled to the name of Clergy, in the only legitimate sense of that term, that is, they are as truly ecclesiastical officers as those who "labour in the word and doctrine."[15]

Miller did not believe he could successfully redefine the word "clergy." He did hope to succeed in discouraging the use of the term "lay elder." He concluded:

> Let all necessary distinction be made by saying:—"Ministers, or pas-tors, Ruling Elders, Deacons, and the Laity, or body of the people."

This will be in conformity with ancient usage. This will be maintaining every important principle. This can offend none; and nothing more will be desired by any.[16]

There is much more of Miller's important book that could be read with great benefit by leaders of today's church.[17] Miller advanced strong arguments for the practice of laying on of hands in the ordaining of ruling elders. He believed that ruling elders should participate in the laying on of hands in the ordination of both ruling elders and deacons because ordination was an act of government, and ruling elders participate in government. He could not, however, go so far as to argue for the participation of ruling elders in the laying on of hands in the ordination of teaching elders. For Miller such a practice was "contrary to essential Presbyterian principle."[18] One additional quotation will have to conclude this discussion of Miller's important work on the subject of the ruling elder:

> The design of appointing persons to the ordered ministry of Ruling Elder is not to pay them a compliment; not to give them an opportunity of figuring as speakers in judicatories; not to create the pageants of ecclesiastical ceremony; but to secure able, faithful, and truly devoted counselors and rulers of the Church; to obtain wise and efficient guides, who shall not only go along with the flock in their journey heavenward, but go before them in everything that pertains to Christian duty.[19]

Parity in Governance

It was not until the latter half of the twentieth century that the complete equality of ruling elders with teaching elders in exercising governance was established in all branches of what has become the Presbyterian Church (U.S.A.). The journey to achieve parity between ruling elders and teaching elders and to grant to the ministry of ruling elder the proper authority and responsibility has been a long one. Further, many Reformed churches in the world today still do not find it necessary to set apart ruling elders and deacons by ordination with the laying on of hands.

It has been a significant contribution of Presbyterianism in the United States to emphasize that the ministry of ruling elder must be accorded the same dignity and respect that is given to the ministry of teaching elder. Future chapters of this book will consider the responsibilities of today's ruling elders, functioning both individually and as members of sessions and more-inclusive governing bodies. This chapter's glimpses into the past have established the importance of the ministry of ruling elder within the Reformed tradition.

Questions for Reflection and Discussion

1. What particular perspectives might ruling elders bring to the governance of the church that teaching elders may not?

2. Does your congregation have a positive climate for the ministry of ruling elders and deacons? What could make it more positive?

3. Ruling elders and deacons are meant to be spiritual leaders in Presbyterian congregations. Do you see yourself as a spiritual leader? Why or why not?

4. If you were responsible to call on a potential nominee for ruling elder, what would you say to them about what the ministry entails in your church?

Chapter Five

THE ORDERED MINISTRY OF DEACON

Nancy Jones attended a conference on the church's mission sponsored by her presbytery. In a small-group discussion Betty Pierce, a member of a church in a nearby town, spoke enthusiastically about the activities of her church's deacons, who reach out in a wide variety of ways to persons in need in the community. Nancy was amazed. Her church had not had any deacons in years and, as far as Nancy knew, her church was doing very little to help the poor or others in need. When Nancy shared her surprise with the group, Bill Green, from the presbytery's largest church, pointed out that the deacons in his church are in charge of promoting stewardship, taking up the offering during worship and counting it after the service, and, of course, ushering. Since these tasks are very demanding ones in his large church, the deacons have almost no time or energy for service in the community. Bill too gained new ideas from what Betty had shared. But by now, everyone in the group had become somewhat confused about just what deacons are supposed to do.

The *Book of Order* [G-2.0201] states:

The ministry of deacon as set forth in Scripture is one of compassion, witness, and service, sharing in the redeeming love of Jesus Christ for the poor, the hungry, the sick, the lost, the friendless, the oppressed, those burdened by unjust policies or structures, or anyone in distress. The Constitution is clear. The primary duty assigned to all deacons is that of ministering to persons in need or in distress. This function is broadly stated to encompass service to any person in need anywhere. No limits of location or of categories of need exist. Second, deacons are to assume any other duties that the session chooses to delegate to them. [G-2.0202]

Many churches have long traditions of the deacons' fulfilling particular functions. The Constitutions of the PCUS and UPCUSA, our two predecessor denominations, listed additional duties to those now specified in the Presbyterian Church (U.S.A.) *Book of Order,* and what the Constitutions did not add, tradition did.

In order to understand some of the current diversity surrounding the role of the deacon—and whether there should even be a separate ordered ministry of deacon—it is necessary to look at the ways in which the ministry of deacon developed and changed within the Reformed tradition, especially in the United States.

The Ordered Ministry of Deacon
in the Reformed Tradition

When in the mid-sixteenth century John Calvin developed a polity for governing the church in Geneva, one of the ministries for which he found a scriptural basis was the ministry of deacon. Calvin turned to the story of the appointing of the seven in the sixth chapter of Acts and saw there deacons who cared for the poor and distributed alms to them. According to Acts, when the apostles heard that some church members felt that the relief of the poor was not being handled fairly, they asked that this part of their work be entrusted to a separate group of seven persons who would not have the responsibility of preaching and so could focus their attention on the work of serving tables. Calvin concluded: "Here, then, is the kind of deacons the apostolic church had, and which we, after their example, should have."[1]

Following Calvin, Presbyterians of Scotland provided for the ordered ministry of deacon in the *First Book of Discipline* of 1560. There was one important difference between Calvin and the Scots, however. Scottish polity permitted deacons to be members of church courts—what we today know as councils. However, by the time the *Second Book of Discipline* was legally enacted by the Acts of Parliament in 1592 Calvin's view predominated in Scotland, and it was specified that deacons were not to be members of any church council.[2]

The 1788 Constitution

The first Constitution of the Presbyterian Church in the United States of America, adopted by the Synod of New York and Philadelphia in 1788, contained a very brief chapter titled "Of Deacons." As was the custom throughout this first Form of Government, Scripture passages were cited to support the constitutional text. These Scripture passages are helpful references for persons today interested in the ordered ministry of deacon. The texts cited are Philippians 1:1; 1 Timothy 3:8–15; Acts 6:1–2; and Acts 6:3, 5–6.

The language of the 1788 Form of Government is itself very helpful for understanding the developing role of the deacon:

Of Deacons

The scriptures clearly point out deacons as distinct officers in the church, whose business it is to take care of the poor, and to distribute among them the collections which may be raised for their use. To them also may be properly committed the management of their temporal affairs in the church. [V]

Other sections of this Form of Government provided for the election and ordination of deacons. As with ruling elders, there was no mention of the laying on of hands in ordination, only the provision that the deacon "shall be set apart, by prayer, to the office . . . and the minister shall give him, and the congregation, an exhortation suited to the occasion" [XII].

A careful reading of these early constitutional provisions makes clear that care of the poor is the primary function of the deacon. To care for the poor involves the distribution of the money collected for their benefit, and this aspect of the deacon's task is specifically mentioned.

In addition to caring for the poor, a second function is mentioned—the management of the church's temporal affairs. It should be noted that this management "may be properly committed" to the deacons. It is not essential to the ministry as is the care of the poor.

Encouraging Churches to Institute
the Ordered Ministry of Deacon

Although the earliest American Presbyterian Constitution recognized deacons as "a distinct office in the church," many congregations did not make use of it. With the renewed interest in polity that developed in the1830s, efforts were made to strengthen the ministry of deacon. The Old School General Assembly on at least three occasions in the 1840s and 1850s urged congregations to appoint deacons. In 1841 the Old School Assembly noted that, in response to the urging of the 1840 Assembly that presbyteries urge their churches to appoint deacons, there was some indication that "to a considerable extent the Presbyteries had taken order on the subject."[3]

Also, throughout the mid-nineteenth century numerous spokespersons published pamphlets and articles in periodicals urging the church to recognize the importance of the office by electing deacons and then admonishing deacons themselves to fulfill their ministry of service. Although the language is clearly that of an earlier day, the reasoning that was used has an amazingly contemporary ring to it.

Of major concern was the intent of the biblical texts concerning the ministry of deacon. Were deacons appointed only for a particular time and place, or should the New Testament references to deacons be understood as important for the church's life in all times and places? Opinions differed: Some viewed the ordered ministry of deacon as perpetual, while others reasoned that only those churches with many poor people among their membership needed to continue the ministry of deacon.

A forceful advocate for the permanency of the ministry was the Reverend James B. Ramsey. In an essay read before the Synod of Virginia in 1858 and later published in pamphlet form, Dr. Ramsey, while acknowledging that the deacon is generally viewed as unimportant in the Presbyterian

Church, proceeds to develop a number of compelling arguments for the importance of the ordered ministry in the ongoing life of the church.

According to Ramsey, the church's obligation to care for the poor rests on more than a general duty of compassion to those who suffer. It rests "on the far stronger grounds of the union of all believers with Christ and with each other."[4] Ramsey uses the language of 1 Corinthians 12: We are all "one body in Christ, and every one members one of another. . . . And whether one member suffer, all the members suffer with it." Ramsey concludes, "The care of the poor, relieving their wants and soothing their sorrows, and encouraging their crushed spirits, is, therefore, a duty entwined in the very nature of the Christian life—springing naturally and necessarily out of the believer's union with Christ."[5]

Ramsey also emphasizes the importance of the church's corporate, ordered response to the service of the poor. It was not enough to trust this crucial task

> to take its chances among individual sympathies. From the very first it was recognized as a church duty, a matter of public arrangement by the whole body. Just as their abundant and spontaneous offerings for such as were in need were the natural expression of the feeling that they were all members one of another, so this official attention to it by the Church, in her organized capacity, was a necessary result of the principle then so deeply and vividly felt, of her unity in Christ.[6]

The care of the poor is a distinct function of the church, and one that demands a corporate, not an individual, response. It is for these reasons that Ramsey advocates understanding the office as perpetual and universal. Ramsey has several answers for those who believe that whenever the care of the poor "can be attended to by the session without interfering with other duties, it is perfectly right to do so, and to dispense with this office until the same exigency arises as in the primitive church." He cites the Acts story and reasons that the apostolic church could have very easily increased the number of elders to care for those in need rather than creating a separate ordered ministry. The work of receiving and disbursing the church's charities "was of such a nature that it was better to be entirely separated from all other duties, and committed to a distinct body of officers—distinct not only from the Apostles themselves, but also from those to whom they had committed the government and teaching."[7]

An additional argument advanced by Ramsey has much relevance for the church of our day. Ramsey recognized that the duties already assigned to the pastor and the ruling elders were so extensive as to make it very difficult for these leaders to perform the duties of deacons as well. "The fact is, that where there are no deacons, and their duties are left to the Session, they are in almost all cases, scarcely performed at all. This whole function of the Church lies paralyzed."[8] As a corollary Ramsey added:

But it may be asked, of what use are deacons to take care of the poor in churches where there are no poor, or but two or three? *That, indeed, is a sadly defective state of the Church where there are no poor;* there must be something very deficient in its zeal and aggressiveness, if amidst the multitudes of poor around us, and mingling with us, there are none in the church itself. . . .

But, even supposing that within the bounds of some particular congregation there are no poor that need the church's aid; still, are there not multitudes of God's poor elsewhere that need aid? And is not such a favored church especially bound to extend her help to the less favored? And outside of the Church—among the ignorant multitudes in our own land, and the impoverished nations of our world, has God not chosen ones to be looked after, sought out and gathered in? And are not such churches especially called upon to go forth on errands of mercy to these—errands like that of Jesus Himself to our poor world—personally to those within their reach, and by their messengers to others?[9]

While Ramsey and others were exhorting churches to institute the ordered ministry of deacon to be the agent of the church's ministry of compassion, an evolution in the understanding of the ministry was also under way. Functions that were at first simply logical extensions of the primary work of the deacon became more and more prominent aspects of the deacon's task. It is easy to see how the emphasis on the deacon as the manager of the church's money could become such a large responsibility as to be viewed as the primary task of the deacons. Unfortunately, over a period of time, that is exactly what happened in many congregations that did use the ordered ministry of deacon.

Recovering the Essence
of the Ordered Ministry of Deacon

The reunion of the PCUS and the UPCUSA in 1983 brought together a variety of traditions surrounding the ministry of deacon. Some congregations of the UPCUSA had no tradition of a diaconate, with all the functions of such a group assumed by the session or by trustees. Some congregations of the PCUS had in recent years exercised their constitutional option of electing not to use the ordered ministry of deacon, with all the responsibilities of a board of deacons falling on the session. Many congregations from both streams of the church had active boards of deacons. But those of the former PCUS came from a tradition where the secondary functions assigned to the diaconate (after the primary function of service to those in need) were all related to stewardship education, financial planning and management, and property management. Diaconates of congregations from the UPCUSA stream had the greatest variety of patterns, since the functions suggested as appropriate for their work extended beyond the areas of stewardship education and financial and property management to more general program responsibility—specifically evangelistic, missionary, and educational programs. These last-mentioned areas of responsibility were more closely related to the primary task of service. Where the management of the church's "temporalities" was delegated to trustees, the church's board of deacons had been free to develop a ministry of service, both directly (that is, performed by the deacons themselves) and by service-related program responsibility in the overall life of the congregation.

Upon reunion, the framers of the *Book of Order* of the Presbyterian Church (U.S.A.) were faced with patterns of church life that lacked a clear understanding of the function of the deacon. How might the essence of the ministry be emphasized, first in the Constitution of the reunited church, and then in its life? The *Book of Order* recovered the distinctiveness that has long eluded the ordered ministry of deacon by stating the nature of the ministry in the simplest possible terms. Churches were free to continue in whatever pattern of effectively using the ministry has been meaningful to them in the past, since sessions may delegate whatever responsibilities they like to the deacons. And churches are also free to discover a new significance in an ordered ministry that perhaps they have combined with the ministry of ruling elder (choosing not to have a separate board of deacons) or which they perhaps have used but in a way that has lacked vitality and creativity.

The constitutional statement of the Presbyterian Church (U.S.A.) pre-2011 makes it very clear why Presbyterians ordain deacons. Deacons are ordained (set into an ordered pattern of church life) for the purpose of "minister[ing] to those who are in need, to the sick, to the friendless, and to any who may be in distress" [G-6.0402, *Book of Order* 2009-2011]. Any other functions deacons serve may be extremely valuable, but they are secondary to the function of service. Deacons are ordained to serve, and not just to serve the church in some administrative function. Deacons are ordained to serve those who are in need, in a very direct and personal way.

The form of service emphasized by deacons will differ according to place and situation. Some churches may focus a large portion of their service on meeting special needs of persons with a disability. The deacons of one church may concentrate on enabling the elderly of their community to experience fuller days, utilizing and sharing their special gifts. Another church's deacons may operate a night shelter for the homeless of a community. The deacons of several churches in a city could join forces in a larger effort to meet specific community needs. The ways of fulfilling the specific responsibility of deacons seem endless.

Reformed churches have placed less emphasis on a liturgical function for deacons than many of our partner churches within the ecumenical church. A major study of ordination presented to the 1992 General Assembly suggests adding a liturgical dimension to the functions of the deacon. Deacons should lead in the portions of the liturgy that most relate to their responsibility for ministries of service to the powerless and others in need, namely reading the gospel lesson, gathering and presenting the gifts of the people, and preparing and assisting in serving the Lord's Supper.[10] This ordination report, after significant study in the church, led to the 1998 amendment adding new responsibility to the ordered ministry of deacon.

The same ordination study also calls for the provision to allow deacons to be individually commissioned by the session and not organized into a board of deacons. According to the study, the core functions of the ministry of deacon all involve following the self-emptying pattern of Christ in service to others either on a one-to-one basis or to particular groups in the church or community. These functions do not require that deacons be organized as a board. Time spent in organizing, planning, and attending meetings can reduce the amount of time and energy for person-to-person service. Also, a limited term of active service, while important in a ministry focusing on decision-making and governance, is not an issue when the ministry focuses on setting an example and persuading others to join in reaching out to persons in need.[11]

Deacons in the Current Form of Government

As we stated at the beginning of this chapter, the current Form of Government specifies that deacons have a special ministry to those in need and in distress of any kind. They are to be "Persons of spiritual character, honest repute, exemplary lives, brotherly and sisterly love, sincere compassion, and sound judgment" [G-2.0201].

Although there is less actual material about the ministry of deacons in the current Form of Government than in the former one, the current section provides great flexibility to congregations. They are free to develop new and creative ways to shape the ministry of deacons in the congregation and beyond.

Under the new Form of Government the door remains open for a congregation to elect one or more persons to the ordered ministry of deacon who would be trained, examined, and ordained by the session and then be commissioned by the session to particular tasks of diaconal ministry. The tasks could possibly be accomplished through the deacon's professional work in such fields as medicine, education, or social work or through volunteer service in a particular ministry. The commissioned deacons may together be involved in a particular project on behalf of the congregation.

The current Form of Government makes it clear that the work of the deacons, whatever shape it takes, is under the oversight and control of the session. Both session and deacons should take this relationship seriously. It is wise for the session to keep in close contact with the work of the deacons and receive regular reports from individual deacons or from the board of deacons.

Congregations are still free to organize their deacons in the way that best suits their ministry. They are also free not to use the ordered ministry of deacon if it is not suitable for that particular congregation. Churches that have chosen not to use the ministry of deacon but rather to have all of the responsibilities of deacons assumed by the session may find it reasonable to review this decision from time to time. As they reassess the congregation's mission and consider how best to accomplish it, one or more of the ways of using the ministry of deacon could become helpful in expanding the church's reach and effectiveness.

It is the responsibility of the session to oversee and lead in all aspects of the church's life. Not so the deacons. They have the advantage of a limited responsibility, with the freedom to concentrate on one task. A church can choose to give to its deacons no duty other than relieving human need. A church can turn the deacons loose to learn, to act, to try and try again, as they search for the most effective ways of fulfilling their ministry of compassion.

Electing and ordaining persons to the ministry of deacon is the way the church seeks to assure in the ordering of its corporate life that the ministry of compassion is never overlooked.

Questions for Reflection and Discussion

1. Does your congregation use the ordered ministry of deacon? If so, how are they helpful to the church in carrying out its mission?

2. If your congregation does not use the ordered ministry of deacon, why not?

3. If your church uses the ordered ministry of deacon, has there ever been friction between deacons and the session? What was the conflict about?

4. What do you think about James Ramsey's comment about churches that have no poor people in them?

Chapter Six

A FIRST LOOK
AT
THE SESSION

The session of Little Chapel Presbyterian Church is struggling with a question that is troubling the members. A new family has been visiting regularly for several months. The two enthusiastic teenagers have invigorated the high school church school class. Their mother has added a much-needed alto voice to the choir. The pastor has visited the family twice, urging them to join the church. They have indicated their interest in doing so. However, the father, an articulate, well-educated person, has made it clear to the pastor and another session member that although a member of the Presbyterian Church for all his adult life, he is not now able to affirm faith in Jesus Christ as Lord and Savior. He would like to transfer his membership to Little Chapel Church with the rest of the family, as long as the session will not ask him any questions. It is the policy of the Little Chapel session to ask every person seeking membership in the congregation to reaffirm the questions asked of those making a profession of faith. The session believes it should continue its policy, but it fears losing a new family, especially this one.

The session of Green Valley Presbyterian Church was taking a look at its membership rolls in order to assure their accuracy. When they came to the name Jane Wilkes, the whole group seemed to be in agreement that she should be placed on the inactive roll. "We haven't seen her in worship or in any of the church's programs for a year or two," remarked one ruling elder. "She has become totally inactive," commented another. Then the pastor asked, "Have we done anything to reach out to her and encourage her to resume active involvement here? Frankly, I forgot about Jane. I called her perhaps two years ago, but I haven't done anything since. Have any of you?"

An Overview of Responsibilities and Powers

The session of every Presbyterian congregation is responsible for governing the congregation and guiding its witness [G-3.0201]. This is a big job! Many duties that might be necessary to carry out these responsibilities are not explicitly stated in the current Form of Government. An outline of things the session might find falling under this responsibility is given below. We hope it will help ruling elders grasp the scope of their duties and think creatively about the ministry to which they have been called, elected, and ordained. The chapters of this book dealing in more detail with the various responsibilities are cited at the right.

Responsibilities and Powers of the Session for the Mission and Government of the Particular Church

I. Equipping the church's members to be evangelists   (chapter 9)
    and providing opportunities for them to share
    their faith with each other and in the world

II. Receiving members into the church   (chapter 6)
    A. Three ways of receiving members
    B. Three categories of membership
    C. Preparing persons for membership and baptism
    D. Keeping accurate rolls and registers

III. Leadership of the congregation in reaching out   (chapter 9)
    A. In participating in the mission of the whole
       church in the world
    B. In ministries of personal and social healing and
       reconciliation within the particular community
    C. In discovering God's activity in the world
       and in planning for change, renewal, and
       reformation under God's Word

IV. Ordering the life of the particular church
    A. Providing for the worship of God's people   (chapter 14)
    B. Developing and supervising the   (chapters 6 and 8)
       education program
    C. Challenging the people with the privilege   (chapter 11)
       of responsible stewardship of money, time,
       and talents
    D. Establishing the annual budget and deter-   (chapter 11)
       mining the distribution of benevolences
    E. Instructing, examining, ordaining,   (chapters 2 and 3)
       installing, and welcoming ruling elders
       and deacons
    F. Delegating and supervising the work   (chapters 6 and 11)
       of deacons, trustees, and all other
       church organizations

G. Providing for the administration of the   (chapter 8)
    church's program, including employment and
    compensation of staff
H. Providing for the management   (chapter 11)
    of the church's property
I. Calling meetings of the congregation when
    appropriate

V.   Responsibility for members and their growth   (chapter 6)
    and equipment for ministry
    A Pastoral care
    B. Sharing in fellowship
    C. Opportunities for witness and service in
        the world
    D. Correcting patterns of discrimination
    E. Supporting inquirers and candidates for teaching
        elder and other professional service
    F. Reviewing with members their   (See also chapter 2)
        fulfillment of membership responsibilities
    J. Encouraging members who have moved
        away from the area to establish
        membership elsewhere

VI.   Responsibility for church leaders   (chapter 6)
    A. Supporting and encouraging the faithfulness
        of ruling elders and deacons in fulfilling
        their responsibilities
    B. Engaging in a process for training and
        spiritual growth of leaders

VII.   Beyond the congregation—relationships with
    other councils, the community, and
    the ecumenical church
    A. Electing or nominating persons to serve   (chapter 10)
        as members of presbytery, synod, and General
        Assembly while paying attention to principles
        of inclusiveness
    B. Observing and carrying out any   (chapter 10)
        constitutional instructions from higher
        governing bodies
    C. Welcoming representatives of presbytery   (chapter 10)
    D. Proposing overtures through presbytery   (chapter 10)
        to the synod or General Assembly
    E. Establishing and maintaining local   (chapter 9)

Gathering the Community of Faith

It is the responsibility of the session to receive members into the church
[G-3.0201c]. This responsibility is assigned to presbytery when a church
is being organized, but as soon as the church is constituted by presbytery
and a session duly elected and installed, the responsibility becomes that
of the session.

The session receives persons into active church membership in three
ways: upon public profession of faith, upon reaffirmation of faith in Jesus
Christ, or upon satisfactory certification of transfer of church membership
[G-1.0303]. More information on this topic is found in the Directory for
Worship section 4.2003–.2004.

Chapter 2 of this book discusses the call of Christ to church membership
and the responsibilities assumed by church members. Here our purpose
is to look at those things sessions must understand in order to fulfill their
role in building up the church through the reception of church members.

It is important for ruling elders to understand that there are three
categories of membership in the Presbyterian Church (U.S.A.). Thus far
we have been talking about *active* members, those persons who present
themselves for membership through profession of faith, reaffirmation
of faith, or transfer of their membership from another congregation. By
presenting herself or himself to the session to become a member of that
particular church, those joining voluntarily submit to the government of
the Presbyterian Church (U.S.A.) and agree to participate actively in the
church's work and worship.

The session, after careful study and discussion with the congregation,
may set conditions of active membership other than those in the Form of
Government, but any such conditions must be consistent with the order
and confessions of the Presbyterian Church (U.S.A.). Perhaps a distinction
should be made between *entering* and *maintaining* membership in a congregation. G-1.0302 makes it clear that the reason for denying membership
to any person must have to do with the profession of faith (or lack of such
a profession). Membership is never to be denied to any person because of
race, economic or social circumstances, or any other reason not related to
profession of faith.

The prior Form of Government made provision for inactive members of the church. These were people who did not participate regularly in the church's work and worship but were still connected and eligible for certain rights and privileges of membership. The current Form of Government makes no provision for this category of membership. Sessions must therefore consider carefully what to do with the persons who were listed on their *inactive* rolls when the new Form of Government took effect. This would be a good time to reach out to these people once more. This outreach could take the form of calls or visits to encourage the inactive members to reconnect with the church at a deeper lever. Those who have moved away can be encouraged to join a church in their new area. A part of maintaining the integrity of the church's membership involves dealing responsibly with persons who are no longer active, for whatever reasons.

Another category of membership is the *affiliate* member. This person is an active member of another congregation of the Presbyterian Church (U.S.A.) or another denomination who is *temporarily* located away from the church of active membership and who desires to be affiliated with a church where active involvement is possible while maintaining membership in the home church. The session receives persons as affiliate members when they present a certificate of good standing from the session of a Presbyterian church or from the appropriate council of a church of another denomination. An affiliate member may participate in the life of the congregation in the same manner as an active member except that an affiliate member may not vote in congregational meetings or be elected to ordered ministry or other office in the congregation" [G-1.0403].

The remaining category of membership is that of the baptized member:

> A baptized member is a person who has received the sacrament of baptism, whether in this congregation or elsewhere, and who has been enrolled as a baptized member by the session but who has not made a profession of faith in Jesus Christ as Lord and Savior. Such baptized members receive the pastoral care and instruction of the church and may participate in the sacrament of the Lord's Supper. [G-1.0401]

Brought by their believing parents or others exercising parental responsibility for them, baptized members generally enter the church's membership as infants or children. In presenting the child for baptism, these parents reaffirm their own faith, claim the covenant promises of God on behalf of the child and promise "to provide nurture and guidance within the community of faith until the child is ready to make a personal profession of faith and assume the responsibility of active church membership" [W-2.3014]. Baptized members become active members at the time that they make a profession of faith in Jesus Christ as Lord and Savior, thereby claiming for themselves the faith in which they were baptized. Those who do not make a profession of faith as adolescents or young adults remain baptized members of the church until such time as they do claim Jesus as Lord and Savior. Baptized members may remain in that category of church membership throughout an entire lifetime.

The session has the extremely important responsibility of preparing persons for entering the community of faith, that is, for becoming church members. This responsibility begins with preparation for baptism [W-2.3012]. If the person being baptized is an infant or young child, then the preparation will be done with the parent(s) or other responsible person(s) presenting the child for baptism. In addition to encouraging parents to present their children for baptism, sessions should remind parents of the meaning of baptism and its significance. They should counsel the parents or persons "rightly exercising parental responsibility" on their role in nurturing the child in the Christian life [W-2.3012b]. As the child grows, the session becomes responsible for nurturing the child "in understanding the meaning of Baptism, of the Lord's Supper, and of their interrelation" [W-2.3012e]. The session's responsibility enlarges as the child develops and grows. The session particularly is charged with exercising the whole congregation's responsibility "to nurture those who are baptized to respond to the invitation to the Lord's Supper. . . . When the child begins to express a desire to receive this Sacrament, the session should take note of this and provide an occasion for recognition and welcome" [W-4.2002].

As the session exercises its responsibility to prepare persons to join the church, it is important to try to make the preparation appropriate for the particular persons who come to unite with the church. A person long inactive in the church but now reaffirming faith in Jesus Christ and picking up once again the responsibilities of membership might well need to receive fairly extensive preparation—perhaps as much as the person professing faith for the first time. A person long an active church member but new to the Presbyterian family might be interested in some special learning opportunities about the Reformed tradition. A person who has been very active as a leader and member of a presbytery council in another part of the country might need to learn only about the mission emphasis of the new congregation and new presbytery.

When taken seriously, the overall responsibility of the session in the membership area—not fully outlined in the Form of Government—is one that requires significant time and effort. The session is responsible for

> seeking out potential members,
> extending the invitation to membership to visitors and newcomers,
> encouraging parents to present their children for baptism,
> nurturing baptized members as they move toward professing their own faith,

instructing those who come to faith and wish to profess it publicly for the first time

providing a meaningful opportunity for them to make their profession before the congregation, and

preparing and counseling those who reaffirm their faith and those who come by transfer of their certificate of membership, giving an opportunity to both for renewing their commitment to Jesus Christ in a service of worship.

Sessions are specifically charged with the responsibility of maintaining accurate rolls of the three categories of church members [G-3.0204]. Only the session, through its clerk, has the right to place new names on the membership rolls or to remove, or delete, names from the rolls. The care that a session gives to its roll-keeping responsibilities shows that session's respect for the church's members and its valuing of the call to church membership.

A Continuing Responsibility for Members

The session of every Presbyterian congregation has an ongoing responsibility for the church's members. The *Book of Order* gives the session special responsibility for nurturing believers. This responsibility covers a wide range of ministry involving "all of life and life's transitions" [W-6.2001–.2003]. Some of these include reviewing the rolls, encouraging stewardship, managing the property of the church, seeing that new leaders are trained and set in their places of service, leading in mission, warning against error in doctrine and practice, and serving in judicial matters when necessary [G-3.0201]. The Directory for Worship highlights Christian nurture as a mutual ministry of church members to one another [W-6.1002–.1003]. Specifically mentioned as occasions important for nurturing are the times of "entering the community of faith," "assuming responsibility in the world," "living out Christian vocation in public, active life," and continuing discipleship "in circumstances offering new limitations and new freedoms" [W-6.2001–.2004].

Christian Education. The Directory for Worship identifies the Service for the Lord's Day, "when the Word is proclaimed and the Sacraments are celebrated," as "the central occasion for nurture in the church" [W-6.2006]. The importance of this statement cannot be overemphasized. The former Directory for the Service of God (which was replaced by the Directory for Worship in 1988) states, "The church institutions created for nurture are primarily the church school and other classes and seminars for education."[1] It is an extremely important development for the *Book of Order* to move from an emphasis on the church school to the Service for the Lord's Day as being central to the educational or nurturing task of the church. Speaking of the Service for the Lord's Day, the Directory for Worship continues: "The session should ensure that regular programs of the church do not prevent children's full participation with the whole congregation in worship, in Word and Sacrament, on the Lord's Day" [W-3.1004].

The Directory for Worship does identify other occasions for nurture provided by the church. The "classes of the church school" and "other groups and fellowships organized for education and nurture" are among the occasions listed [W-6.2006a, b]. The session needs to be certain that these programs are designed to enable the growth and equipment for ministry of all the church's members. The session must think about the various age groups that make up the church. It must not forget those persons who have disabilities, both mental and physical. The session should also seek to provide educational opportunities for the growing number of single persons of all ages who are a part of the church family. Sessions that find that their church has very few persons in one particular age group need to look closely at the intergenerational learning materials that are now available. The fact that a church has only one or two children in a particular age group does not relieve the session of the responsibility to provide some meaningful experience of spiritual nurture for them.

Inclusiveness. Closely related to the concern for personal growth of members is the responsibility placed on the session, as on all other councils, to fulfill the church's commitment to inclusiveness in diversity. As the session cares for the church's members it must constantly ask who has been excluded from "full participation and representation in [the church's] worship, governance and emerging life" [F-1.0403].

We have earlier mentioned the question of inclusiveness relating to the election of church leaders. What about other areas of the church's life? How accessible are the church buildings? Can a person in a wheelchair participate fully in the church's worship and program? Look over the membership lists of session committees. Are they inclusive of a wide variety of ages? Are the young people in the church asked to assume some responsibilities that contribute to the life of the whole church? Does the church find ways to use the tremendous gifts of time and talent that its retired members have to offer? Are persons of races other than the majority one really included in the life of the congregation? Do they have the opportunity to share the gifts they bring from their racial ethnic heritage? Sessions need to ask these hard questions regularly and to develop strategies for continuing progress in making the church more inclusive in its total life.

Candidates for Professional Service. Another responsibility of the session toward the church's members is that of supporting those who explore the possibility of becoming inquirers (and later candidates) for the ordered ministry of teaching elder or for other professional service in the church. The main responsibility for inquirers and candidates is lodged in the presbytery. However, persons seeking to enter into a covenant relationship with presbytery as inquirers for the ministry of the Word and Sacrament "shall have received the endorsement of the sponsoring congregation [G-2.0602].

In G-2.0601 we see that "those who are to be ordained as teaching elders receive full preparation for their task under the direction of the presbytery." For this purpose the sponsoring session and congregation enter into a covenant relationship with the candidate and the presbytery. The session has the same responsibilities toward an inquirer or a candidate as toward any other church member. In addition, the session's concern includes providing support—both emotional and financial, if needed—for the person's preparation for ministry. It is wise for the session to appoint a member of the congregation to serve as a liaison with the inquirer or candidate, although this is not required in the Form of Government.

Members Reviewing Their Membership Responsibilities. One of the duties of church members is to take the initiative in "reviewing and evaluating regularly the integrity of one's membership, and considering ways in which one's participation in the worship and service of the church may be increased and made more meaningful" [G-1.0304]. The session can be very helpful by providing encouragement and structure to members for this process. Perhaps at the same time that members are evaluating for themselves their fulfillment of the responsibilities entrusted to them as members, the session might review how well it has fulfilled its responsibilities for the growth and development of the church's members.

Deleting Names from Rolls. The Form of Government specifies circumstances when the session may or shall delete the names of persons from the various rolls of the church [G-3.0204a]. A person's name shall be removed when he or she dies, when the member joins another church or presbytery, or if a member renounces the jurisdiction of the church. A member may be removed from the active roll when that person requests that his or her membership be terminated. This request should be granted only after the session makes a sincere effort to persuade the member to stay. When a member requests that her or his membership be transferred to another church, that person's name is deleted from the roll by the session. This usually happens after notice is received that the member has actually been received into membership in the other church.

The process of receiving members by transfer from one church to another is simplified if the receiving church accepts someone into membership pending receipt of the certificate of transfer. Then the person has already been received when the transferring session receives notice of the request for transfer, and it can delete the person's name immediately. Whenever a session issues a certificate of transfer for parents of young children, it is a good practice to include on the certificate the names of the children and whether they have received the sacrament of baptism. When certificates are issued for ruling elders and deacons they should include the record of ordination. Finally, a member may be removed from the active roll when he or she has not participated in the worship and mission of the congregation for two years. The Form of Government requires that diligent efforts be made to restore the person, including written notice, before removing them from the active roll.

Some readers may be puzzled by all this complexity surrounding transferring membership and deleting persons' names from various rolls. Remember that Presbyterians have a very high view of church membership. That valuing of membership leads us to be very careful as we transfer and terminate membership in particular churches. The Constitution also provides for what happens to members when a church is dissolved by presbytery. In that situation the presbytery assumes jurisdiction over the church's members until it grants them certificates of transfer to other congregations [G-3.0301c]. The person's membership is not "lost" but preserved in the presbytery.

A Continuing Responsibility for Church Leaders

Along with the session's responsibility for "training, examining, ordaining, and installing those elected by the congregation as ruling elders and deacons" [G-3.0201c] is the responsibility to hold them accountable for fulfilling their obligations. Ruling elders and deacons, along with teaching elders, promise at the time of ordination (and again whenever installed for a new term of service) to fulfill their ministry in obedience to Jesus Christ and to "seek to serve the people with energy, intelligence, imagination, and love" [W-4.4003h]. When ruling elders are not taking these commitments seriously, the session should counsel with them about this matter. Actually the session should regularly support and encourage all ruling elders and deacons to be faithful in fulfilling their ministries.

The session, with the pastor, should also take responsibility for engaging in a process of nurture, presumably ongoing, so that leaders may grow spiritually and the whole session and diaconate can discern God's will. The session is responsible for its own continuing education and spiritual nurture! If this important responsibility is neglected, then many of the others assigned to the session will also suffer. A strong experience of Christian nurture and spiritual growth equips people to engage in God's mission in the world with more vigor and discernment. Ruling elders and deacons are also in need of this equipping and care. Stagnant, burned-out leaders cannot lead a vital congregation.

Questions for Reflection and Discussion

1. Which of the tasks of the session do you think are most important to the life of the congregation?

2. How did you come into the congregation as a member? How was the session involved?

3. Has the session of your congregation ever run into problems while trying to remove persons from the rolls? What were the problems? How were they handled?

4. What kind of program or event can you imagine where the session might help church members review how well they are fulfilling the responsibilities of membership?

Chapter Seven

TEACHING ELDERS
SERVING
CONGREGATIONS

A growing suburban church was exploring the possibility of calling its first associate pastor to assume a portion of the increasing responsibilities facing the pastor. Then the church suddenly found itself in a different situation. The pastor who had served so faithfully for the past eight years accepted a call to a church in another part of the country. During an initial meeting of the session with representatives of presbytery's committee on ministry, a member of the committee commented casually that the church's present needs might best be met by a clergy couple serving as co-pastors. The session members looked puzzled. Then the presbytery representative explained that the church now, in effect, had two vacancies at once. One option was the traditional one of calling first a pastor and then an associate. The other was the newer one of calling co-pastors with equal responsibility. At the congregational meeting to elect a pastor nominating committee, the task of the committee could be stated in such a way as to leave the committee free to seek the best pastoral leadership. The session members left that meeting with many new ideas.

The congregation of Dry Canyon Church had recently requested presbytery to dissolve the relationship between the congregation and its pastor of only two and one-half years. The pastor at first did not concur in the request, but after meeting with presbytery's committee on ministry, finally decided that the pastoral relationship was irreparably broken. Presbytery did dissolve the relationship. Several session members began talking immediately about electing a nominating committee to seek another pastor. After meeting with the committee on ministry, however, the majority of the members saw the wisdom in following presbytery's advice. Presbytery had suggested that the church call an interim pastor to help them through their transition. Perhaps Dry Canyon Church even then should not think about calling another pastor full-time. Other possibilities should be considered. For now one thing was clear: Members of Dry Canyon Church needed some more time to rethink the church's mission and to heal the wounds caused by their difficult experience with their previous pastor. All agreed that the church would benefit from the leadership of an interim pastor.

Presbyterians have long emphasized the importance of highly educated teaching elders. Certain responsibilities in the life of the congregation are assigned to the pastor alone. Others are the responsibility of the session, of which the pastor is a member and the moderator. It is extremely important to consider the role of the pastor in the overall life of the particular church, but first it is necessary to take a closer look at the ordered ministry of teaching elder as set forth in the *Book of Order.*

The Ordered Ministry of Teaching Elder

As the Lord has set aside through calling certain members to be teaching elders, so the church confirms that call through the action of the presbytery. The presbytery shall determine whether a particular work may be helpful to the church in mission and is a call to a validated ministry requiring ordination as a teaching elder. In the performance of that ministry, the teaching elder shall be accountable to the presbytery. Teaching elders have membership in the presbytery by action of the presbytery itself, and no pastoral relationship may be established, changed, or dissolved without the approval of the presbytery. [G-2.0502]

The presbytery is the council that has jurisdiction over teaching elders. The church through the presbytery (G-2.0502) confirms the call of persons to this special form of ministry and approves their involvement in any specific work. Serving in a pastoral relationship to a particular church is only one of many specific tasks teaching elders perform that advance the church's witness and mission. Other possible forms of service include educators, chaplains, pastoral counselors, campus teaching elders, missionaries, partners in mission, evangelists, administrators, social workers, and consultants.

All teaching elders hold membership in a presbytery, never in a congregation. All teaching elders are accountable to their presbytery. They may also be accountable to a variety of other persons or groups, both within the church and beyond the church. For example, a hospital chaplain is accountable to the hospital for which he or she works, as well as to the presbytery.

In addition to the specific work to which they are called, all teaching elders have some responsibility for participating in the larger ministry of the church. For teaching elders serving congregations this responsibility involves them in the overall work and mission of presbytery and, at certain times, in the ministry of synod and General Assembly. Ecumenical involvement is also encouraged. Sessions and congregations need to understand that the pastor has this responsibility to wider governing bodies and to the ecumenical church and to encourage the pastor to be active in this work. Pastor and session should discuss together the appropriate amount of time and energy that the pastor will expend in service to the larger church. For teaching elders serving presbytery, synod, or the General Assembly, and those in other specialized ministries, participation in the larger ministry of the church includes involvement not only in the work of other councils but also in the life of a particular congregation.

Continuing Members of Presbytery

All teaching elders are continuing members of a presbytery, but their category of membership in that presbytery may differ. They may be engaged in a validated ministry, or be members-at-large, or honorably retired [G-2.0503]. In order to be engaged in a validated ministry, a teaching elder must be involved in a work that meets the standards developed by the presbytery for validation of ministries within its bounds. The requirements for validated ministries are found in G-2.0503a. Validated ministries may be in any number of settings. Because of its scope and purpose, this book will focus its attention on those validated ministries that are in particular congregations.

Those engaged in validated ministries have the right to take part in presbytery meetings and to speak, vote, and hold office in a council. These same rights are also explicitly extended to members-at-large. A *member-at-large* is defined as "a teaching elder who has previously been engaged in a validated ministry, and who now, without intentional abandonment of the exercise of ministry, is no longer engaged in a ministry that complies with all the criteria in G-2.0503a [G-2.0503b]. The important phrase here is "without intentional abandonment of the exercise of ministry." The intent of this provision is to allow those teaching elders who, for a wide variety of reasons, are between calls to a specific service to maintain their involvement in presbytery. The fulfillment of family responsibilities is specifically cited as one reason for member-at-large status. Even though they are not engaged in a work that meets all the criteria for a validated ministry, members-at-large retain all the rights of active members within the presbytery. Many members-at-large have even more time for service on presbytery committees and in presbytery mission endeavors than those who are active members. The member-at-large is instructed to comply with as many of the five criteria for validated ministries as possible and is encouraged to participate actively in a congregation.

Permanent Pastoral Relationships

A teaching elder can serve a congregation in a variety of pastoral relations. The permanent pastoral relations are pastor, co-pastor, and associate pastor [G-2.0504]. Pastors, co-pastors, and associate pastors are elected by the vote of the congregation with the presbytery actually establishing the relationship between the teaching elder and the congregation. The process of calling the pastor by the congregation and the presbytery's role in examining the teaching elder (if the teaching elder comes from another presbytery), approving the call, and installing the teaching elder are discussed in chapters 2 and 3 of this book. The installed pastor of a church is expected to fulfill all the functions of a pastor to that congregation unless there is a co-pastor or an associate pastor. If so, certain of the pastoral responsibilities may be assigned to the co-pastor or associate pastor at the direction of the session with presbytery's approval [G-2.0504a].

Co-pastors are teaching elders who are called and installed with equal responsibility for pastoral ministry. Each co-pastor is considered a pastor of the church. The way they share their responsibilities within the church must be agreed on with the session and must be approved by the presbytery. When two pastors serve together as co-pastors and one of them leaves the position, the other remains as pastor of the church [G-2.0504a].

Associate pastors are called by the congregation through the pastoral nominating committee process with presbytery's oversight. They are called to perform certain pastoral functions as assigned by the session. To avoid confusion as to what these functions are it helps to make a specific job description part of the associate pastor's call. The call of the associate pastor is not dependent on that of the pastor. When the pastor leaves, the associate pastor may leave or stay as he or she wishes.

Associate pastors are installed by the presbytery and their terms of call must meet the standards of the Form of Government and the presbytery [G-2.0804]. They serve as full voting members of session and may moderate the session on invitation of the pastor.

An associate pastor is not generally permitted to receive the permanent call as the next installed pastor. The reason for this prohibition is to protect the congregation's freedom to choose its own leaders, specifically its pastors. Without such a provision, any congregation that was extremely pleased with the ministry of an associate pastor could place the pastor nominating committee under considerable pressure to call that person to the permanent position. It is the view of the PC(USA) that preserving the pastor nominating committee's right to conduct a thorough and open search outweighs the benefits of permitting an associate pastor to become pastor. The Form of Government does provide an exception to this restriction by a three-fourths vote of the presbytery [G-2.0504c].

Dissolving Permanent Pastoral Relationships

Since presbytery actually establishes the relationship between any installed pastor and the congregation, presbytery must dissolve that relationship [G-2.0901]. The initiative for dissolving the pastoral relationship may come from the teaching elder or from the congregation. If the teaching elder initiates the request, the request must be made to the session which then calls a congregational meeting to consider the matter and vote whether to agree or disagree with the request. This congregational meeting is mandatory.

When a congregation initiates the request, then concurrence is sought from the teaching elder. When teaching elder and congregation concur in requesting that the relationship be dissolved, then the presbytery itself may dissolve the relationship. When the teaching elder and congregation are not in concurrence, the presbytery shall hear the nonconcurring party. After that hearing, presbytery makes its decision, taking into account the total situation. When a presbytery finds that "the church's mission under the Word imperatively demands it," the presbytery may take the initiative to dissolve the pastoral relationship [G-2.0904]. Before taking this action, the pastor, the session, and the congregation must be consulted.

Designated Pastoral Relationships

Designated pastoral relationships are an in-between category of relationships between a teaching elder and a congregation. They are not permanent ones in that they are for a limited period of time. However, designated relationships are technically not temporary ones, since by definition a temporary pastoral relationship involves neither a formal call issued by a congregation nor a formal installation.

A designated pastor is a teaching elder designated by presbytery after consulting with the congregation [G-2.0504a]. The congregation votes to call the designated pastor for the limited time period. Then the presbytery confirms the relationship and installs the designated pastor. The only designated pastoral relationships are pastor and co-pastor.

Some congregations and presbyteries have found the designated pastor relationship helpful in situations where there has been conflict or where the congregation is experiencing some other kind of difficulty. In such cases the designated pastor process provides a method of pastoral service to congregations without the delay of a search process to secure a permanent pastor. Also, use of the designated pastor relationship has freed up congregations to "try out" a pastoral relationship for a set term to see if it is a "fit." A designated pastor may be called as the permanent pastor of the church, just as a stated supply may be. In fact, a frequent hope in establishing the relationship of designated pastor is that the relationship will work out so well that the congregation will want to make it permanent.

Temporary Pastoral Relationships

There are many cases when for one reason or another a church may not have an installed or designated pastor. In these situations the presbytery works with the congregation to find temporary pastoral leadership. The titles and terms of service of such relationships are established by the presbytery as it sees fit. Such titles might include interim pastor, stated supply, and temporary supply. The Form of Government provides that teaching elders, ruling elders, and candidates for ministry are eligible to serve in temporary pastoral relationships. When such a relationship is established, no formal call is issued, and there is no formal installation [G-2.0504b].

When a church finds itself without a pastor, it is a common practice for the presbytery to help the church secure a temporary pastor until a new installed pastor can be called. This person is often called an *interim pastor*. He or she is invited by the session of a church seeking a pastor to help the church get ready to receive new leadership. Depending on the situation and the person involved, the interim may also preach the Word, administer the Sacraments, moderate the session, and fulfill other pastoral duties for a specified period not to exceed twelve months at a time [G-2.0504b].

A minister serving as interim pastor for a congregation that is seeking to fill the position on a permanent basis is not generally permitted to receive the permanent call as the next installed pastor. The reason for this prohibition is the same as mentioned above in the case of associate pastors. Without such a provision the pastor nominating committee might be placed under considerable pressure to call that person to the permanent position. Again, the Form of Government does provide an exception to this restriction by a three-fourths vote of the presbytery [G-2.0504c].

A church may secure a teaching elder, a candidate, or a ruling elder engaged by the session with presbytery's approval, to perform the functions of a pastor in a church that is not seeking an installed pastor. This person is often called a *stated supply pastor*. The relation shall be established only by the presbytery and shall extend for a period not to exceed twelve months at a time.

Some churches are served by the same stated supply for many years. In these situations it becomes difficult to see much difference between the stated supply and an installed pastor. In many small churches stated supplies serve part-time, some only leading worship, moderating the session, and providing pastoral care. The real difference is the way the relationship between the church and the stated supply pastor comes about. The installed pastor is called by the congregation through a pastor nominating

committee. The stated supply is invited to serve by the session with presbytery's approval. After reviewing the stated supply's performance over
the preceding year, the session or presbytery may choose not to renew the
relationship. The *Book of Order* does not place any restriction on a stated
supply's becoming the elected permanent pastor of a church.

Another possible temporary pastoral relationship is that of *temporary
supply*. A temporary supply may be a teaching elder, a candidate, or a ruling elder secured by the session to conduct services for a brief time when
there is no pastor or the pastor is unable to perform pastoral duties. Before
securing such a person to provide pastoral services to the congregation,
the session must seek the approval of presbytery. The Form of Government gives a great deal of room for congregations to use these and other
temporary pastoral services as best suits their needs and mission. The key
provision is that there be conversation between the session and presbytery
as the relationship is worked out.

Another pattern of pastoral leadership for congregations is to call a
ruling elder commissioned by the presbytery to serve as pastor. The presbytery
makes the call as to whether or not using this type of leadership best fur-
thers its mission [G-2.1001]. The commissioned ruling elder works under
presbytery's supervision and is assigned a mentor [G-2.1004]. Presbytery
may grant the commission to a ruling elder to serve as pastor for up to
three years, will review how it is going annually, and may renew or terminate it at any time [G-2.1004].

Ruling elders serving as commissioned pastors receive training by the
presbytery and then are examined as presbytery sees fit as to their personal
faith, their understanding of what they have received in their training, and
in their motives for seeking the call to pastoral service. When presbytery
is satisfied with the applicant's qualifications, he or she is asked the questions found in W-4.4003.

Through this wide variety of pastoral relationships between a teaching
elder and a congregation and, in some cases between an inquirer, a candidate, or a ruling elder and a congregation, the Presbyterian Church (U.S.A.)
seeks to assure that every church has leadership with at least some degree of
training to preach the Word, lead worship, and give pastoral care.

The Distinctive Role of the Pastor

There are certain responsibilities that are so much a part of the work of
the pastor as to be essential for all persons who serve congregations,
unless another teaching elder is also serving the same congregation
and assuming some of these functions. When we speak of the pastor in
this section, we will not be distinguishing between the types of pastoral
relationships. The word "pastor" is used to refer to the entire pastoral
role—those functions that Presbyterian polity assigns to teaching elders

who serve particular congregations in any pastoral capacity, whether temporary, designated, or permanent.

The foundational passage of the Form of Government referring to the pastoral relationship is G-2.0504, an important passage in the *Book of Order.* It says that teaching elders and others duly called into pastoral relationships with congregations "are to be responsible for a quality of life and relationships that commend the gospel to all persons and that communicate its joy and its justice. They are responsible for studying, teaching, and preaching the Word, for celebrating Baptism and the Lord's Supper, and for praying with and for the congregation." The passage continues to describe other responsibilities of the pastor within the congregation, but they are responsibilities that the pastor shares with the ruling elders or deacons. Only those responsibilities quoted above are singled out as the particular responsibility of pastors.

According to the Form of Government, the pastor's task of communicating the gospel cannot be separated from living it. The daily life of the pastor matters. The quality of the pastor's life and the interpersonal relationships that the pastor develops must themselves witness to the gospel and its power to bring joy and establish justice. The relationships that the pastor establishes with members of the church are foundational for any long-term, significant communication. When the pastor lives the gospel and establishes significant relationships, then the pastor's preaching and teaching can be heard.

The pastor is the primary person responsible for studying, preaching, and teaching the Word within the congregation. It is to this task that the teaching elder is ordained and from which the ordered ministry receives its name. Teaching elders are not the only persons within the church who can and should study, preach, and teach the Word, but they are uniquely equipped through theological education. Congregational expectations should allow the pastor adequate time for preparation for preaching and teaching. The pastor who brings fresh insights into preaching and teaching must engage in disciplined study.

Another foundational task of pastors is that of "praying with and for the congregation" [G-2.0504]. The Directory for Worship includes "the prayers offered on behalf of the people and those prepared for the use of the people in worship" among the pastor's responsibilities that are not subject to the authority of the session [W-1.4005a(3)].

The above-quoted passage describes the pastor's praying *with* the congregation in public worship. However, it should be emphasized that G-2.0504 also places on the pastor the responsibility of praying *for* the congregation. It can be a source of great strength to a congregation and to individual members to know that their pastor regularly prays for them.

The congregation and the session need to recognize the importance of the teaching elder's setting aside time for prayer and the ongoing development of his or her own relationship with God.

Teaching elders are leaders of the church set aside through calling and training to perform special functions in the life of the church. These functions center on proclaiming the Word through preaching and the sacraments. Teaching elders are members of presbytery, designated by the presbytery to a particular work. Teaching elders serve congregations in a variety of pastoral relationships, some permanent and some temporary. However, all these pastoral relationships have a great deal in common, for the essential tasks of the pastor should be fulfilled in every congregation. Teaching elders, ruling elders, and candidates in this role must, by the quality of their lives and the relationships formed with the congregation, communicate the gospel, its joy and its justice. They do this through studying, teaching, and preaching the Word, through administering the sacraments, and through praying with and for the people.

Questions for Reflection and Discussion

1. What kinds of pastoral leadership have you experienced? How did each one help the church in its particular situation and mission?

2. The presbytery plays a major role in the calling of pastors to churches. Given what you have read so far in this book, why would you say this is so?

3. Have you ever served on a pastor nominating committee? What was it like?

4. How does your congregation engage in evaluating the pastor or pastor's job performance? How often do these evaluations take place?

Chapter Eight

LEADERS
AND STAFF
WORKING TOGETHER

A new pastor had been at Flat Prairie Presbyterian Church for a few months when members of the session began hearing complaints from some of the church members that the pastor frequently used translations of the Bible different from the pew Bible. Previous pastors had never used any other version. The ruling elders discussed the situation among themselves. One pointed out that the session had no right to instruct the pastor in such matters. The pastor spent three years in seminary studying the Bible, even learning both Hebrew and Greek. The pastor was clearly the best-qualified person to determine which translation of a given Scripture passage was most helpful for use in the congregation's worship. Another person suggested that the ruling elders should inform the pastor of the dissatisfaction that was beginning to develop. Then the pastor could seek the best ways to alleviate the situation, perhaps conferring with the session.

The secretary of Winding Creek Presbyterian Church was visiting a friend. They were discussing problems related to their jobs. The church secretary, not a member of the Presbyterian Church, commented, "If I only understood what things other staff members were responsible for it would make my job so much easier. And it would help to know when certain things have to be completed. I do pretty well keeping up with my work, but sometimes I don't understand the big picture. I feel that we have two pastors, a director of education, and a music director all running around frantically doing a variety of things, but I can't figure out who does what, and I'm not sure they know!"

How can church leaders best work together for the well-being of the church they serve? How can the leaders work with any staff that the session may have employed in addition to the pastor? The roles of the different leaders are distinct and yet interlocking. How can the church's leaders best work together, and with all employed staff, for the building up of the church?

Pastors and Ruling Elders Working Together

The Form of Government, after outlining the special functions of the pastor, continues:

> With the ruling elders, [pastors] are to encourage the people in the worship and service of God; to equip and enable them for their tasks within the church and their mission in the world; to exercise pastoral care, devoting special attention to the poor, the sick, the troubled, and the dying; to participate in governing responsibilities, including leadership of the congregation in implementing the principles of participation and inclusiveness in the decision-making life of the congregation, and its task of reaching out in concern and service to the life of the human community as a whole. [G-2.0504]

The list of responsibilities the pastor shares with the ruling elders is longer than the list that is assigned to the pastor alone. This fact can lead to only one conclusion: It is the intent of Presbyterian polity that pastors and ruling elders work together. When communication breaks down between ruling elders and pastors and when they do not support and supplement each other in their work of ministry, then something is seriously wrong within the life of the congregation. Open communication and mutual respect are the keys to effective service. Pastors and ruling elders must be able to share not only ideas but also concerns with one another, both in one-to-one conversations and in meetings of the session.

Joint Responsibilities for Worship

Pastors and ruling elders together are charged with encouraging the people in the worship and service of God. "Encourage" is a very positive verb. It contains the ideas of motivating, lifting up, challenging, inspiring. The word "encourage" suggests much more than simply telling people to do something or admonishing them for not doing it. To encourage is to enable the people to "lift [their] drooping hands and strengthen [their] weak knees" (Heb. 12:12) so that they may indeed worship and serve their God.

The overall responsibility of making certain that a well-ordered opportunity for worship is available to the congregation lies with the whole session, including, of course, the pastor, who is a member of that session. If there is no pastor, then the session must make provision for a regular worship opportunity, including Word and Sacrament, working closely with the presbytery to assure the best leadership possible [G-3.0201a, b].

The pastor has the particular responsibility for the selection of Scripture, the sermon topic, the prayers, the selection of music, and the use of art forms in worship [W-1.4005a]. The sequence and proportion of various parts of the worship service are determined by the pastor with the agreement of the session. However, arranging for the congregation's worship life is too important a responsibility to be left to any one individual. It is a corporate responsibility of the church's session.

Among the specific worship-related responsibilities of the session are general oversight and approval of public worship; determining days, times, and places of worship; authorizing special services; supervising the music and arts program; authorizing baptisms; determining when the sacrament of the Lord's Supper will be celebrated; and authorizing special offerings for particular purposes [W-1.4004].

Joint Responsibilities for Congregational Care

Returning to G-2.0504, we are reminded that the pastor, with the ruling elders, is assigned the responsibility "to exercise pastoral care, devoting special attention to the poor, the sick, the troubled, and the dying." The responsibility of the session for the continuing care for the congregation is discussed at length in chapter 6 of this book. Here the important point to emphasize is the *corporate nature* of caring for God's people. The responsibility is assigned to ruling elders as well as to pastors. Ruling elders are to perform individual acts of caring for the people of the congregation, giving special attention to those with special needs. It is the joining together of many individual acts of care that helps people experience the church as the body of Christ. The pastor has received special training that should enable him or her to be of particular help in many difficult situations, but this expertise in no way takes the place of the ongoing care provided by the church's ruling elders, deacons, and other members.

As part of their pastoral care responsibilities for the congregation, the congregation's teaching elders, ruling elders, and deacons (also Certified Christian Educators) are required to report any knowledge of child abuse to both church and civil legal authorities. This is a mandatory provision of the Form of Government and must be taken by church leaders to be their Christian duty as well as the duty of their ordered ministry. The "knowledge" referred to in this provision [G-4.0302] relates to "harm, or risk of harm, related to the physical abuse, neglect, and/or sexual molestation or abuse of a minor or an adult who lacks mental capacity." The possibility of such reporting may involve an understanding of the boundaries of confidential communications. Any leader or staff member who believes that they have knowledge they may be required to report should carefully study the confidentiality provisions of G-4.0301. If the leader or staff member reasonably believes that there is risk of future abuse or physical harm, they are obliged to report [G-4.0302].

Joint Responsibilities for Governance

One of the basic responsibilities of teaching elders serving as pastors is to participate in governing responsibilities, along with the ruling elders

[G-2.0504]. The responsibility of the pastor is "with the ruling elders . . . to participate in governing responsibilities, including leadership of the congregation in implementing the principles of participation and inclusiveness in the decision-making life of the congregation" [G-2.0504]. The responsibility of assuming a leadership role in helping their congregations act on the principles of participation and inclusiveness is placed on all pastors.

Pastors and ruling elders together are to take the initiative in helping congregations to understand the commitment of the Presbyterian Church (U.S.A.) to include all groups of its members in the church's decision-making processes. This responsibility includes the breaking down of any barriers that keep church members from full service and participation. Pastors are called on to lead their people to new understandings, new recognitions of the worth of all God's people, and new actions of inclusiveness.

Pastors, Deacons, and Ruling Elders Working Together

When a church has deacons and the deacons are organized into a board, it is customary for the pastor to serve as an advisory member of that board. The board of deacons elects its own moderator and secretary. Pastors are to use their theological and pastoral expertise in advising the board about its particular responsibilities for ministering to persons in need or distress. They are also to become directly involved in the ministries of compassion, sharing with the deacons in meeting human need.

The board of deacons (again, deacons may be individuals commissioned for particular service and not organized into a board), like all other organizations within the church, operates under the jurisdiction of the session. The board of deacons is not a council. Like other church organizations, the board of deacons submits its records to the session, which can void or amend any of the board's actions or direct it to reconsider any decision. However, the session should generally focus its attention on encouraging the board of deacons in their work. It is wise for the session and board of deacons to meet together from time to time to consider matters of joint interest.

In addition to its fundamental responsibility of engaging in a ministry of compassion, the board of deacons is to assume whatever duties may be delegated to it by the session. If the session delegates additional duties to a board of deacons, which is to carry out these duties for and in place of the session, good communication between the session and the board of deacons becomes even more critical. Many churches have chosen not to use a separate ministry of deacon but to have the ruling elders acting individually and the session acting corporately to fulfill the functions of the ministry of deacon. Some congregations that have made this decision have done so because the two bodies of leaders had difficulty working together. In order for each body of leaders to support and enrich the other, good communication and a mutual respect for the God-given gifts and functions of each body must be present. Pastors can do much to foster communication and respect between these two groups of leaders.

Staff Relationships within the Church

In addition to the church's leaders—teaching elders, ruling elders, and deacons—many churches hire staff persons to carry out vital functions in the life of the church. It is extremely important that the contributions of staff members be affirmed, that communication be open between the session, the deacons, and the church's employed staff, and that staff and leaders understand the interrelatedness of their tasks.

For the purposes of this discussion, we will be speaking of all teaching elders who serve a congregation in any official pastoral relationship as members of the staff. As pointed out previously, installed pastors are not employed by the session or the congregation. The presbytery is a necessary partner in establishing any pastoral relationship. Pastors, co-pastors, and associate pastors are included among the church's leaders. But for the remainder of this chapter it is helpful to think in terms of the relationships between ruling elders and deacons as leaders on the one hand, and staff members, including pastors, on the other.

The *Book of Order* says very little about the relationships among the various members of the church staff. It does specify that when the staff includes co-pastors they have equal responsibility for pastoral ministry. The way they share the pastoral duties within the congregation is to be agreed on by the session and approved by the presbytery [G-2.0504a]. When the staff includes associate pastors, their duties are also specified by the session with the approval of presbytery.

To say more about the relationships among particular staff members quickly takes us beyond the *Book of Order*. However, in exercising its overall supervisory role for the governance and mission of the church, the session is responsible for seeing that the staff team works well together. A poorly functioning staff that lacks mutual respect, open and frequent communication, and a clear understanding of their various responsibilities does much to hamper the church's mission and program. Sessions should encourage pastors to hold regular staff meetings, some including the entire employed staff and others for staff members who share particular responsibilities and concerns. The session cannot assume that staff concerns are the responsibility of the pastor alone. If problems develop within the staff of the church, the session should do everything in its power to improve relationships and develop better patterns of communication.

ie Session's Personnel Responsibilities

inciple of leaving as many organizational decisions as ouncil involved, the *Book of Order* does not specify how rsonnel function is to be fulfilled. Many sessions choose to ru.... onsibility through a session personnel committee. The *Book of Order* aoc. lift up several aspects of the personnel function for special attention. One of these is the annual review of the pastor's compensation [G-2.0804]. Another personnel function is concern for equal employment opportunity [G-3.0103].

Our Constitution stresses the principles of inclusiveness and diversity [F-1.0403]. The witness of congregations is the basis for all other expressions of the church's life. Each congregation is responsible to implement its procedures of calling, recruiting, hiring, and promoting without regard to racial ethnic group, sex, age, disability, or marital status. Extending equal employment opportunity to all persons is one way the church lives its faith and bears witness to the community.

The image of the church as Christ's body reminds us that each part of the church must fulfill its special function in order for the body to be healthy and whole. Ruling elders and deacons must perform those particular tasks committed to them. Teaching elders must fulfill their special calling in the life of the church. Other members of the church staff have their particular responsibilities to carry out. All leaders, staff, and members must work together, supporting and encouraging each other so that the church can fulfill Christ's mission.

Questions for Reflection and Discussion

1. Which qualities make for good working relationships among church leaders and staff?

2. Do you have policies in your congregation for handling problems between staff members?

3. How often are staff members, including the pastor(s), evaluated in your church? How effective is this evaluation?

4. What one thing would help the leaders and staff of your congregation work better together?

Chapter Nine

LEADING THE CHURCH
IN MISSION

Sam Washington was asked to serve on his church's evangelism committee, but he confessed to the ruling elder who called him that he had very little enthusiasm for this area of the church's work. "The word 'evangelism' brings to mind people preaching on street corners or making door-to-door calls. Those kinds of things make me uncomfortable."

The pastor of Dunscomb Presbyterian Church reported to the session that a paper on economic justice had been sent out by the General Assembly for study in the churches, and he asked their advice as to how the study might best be carried out. After some discussion, one ruling elder said, "I don't see why we should be studying economics at all. That seems pretty secular to me. Why can't we leave that kind of thing to the experts and get on with our own business?"

Jane Perry and Dan Moore were riding home together after a meeting of their church's mission committee. "I am getting discouraged," said Jane. "We spend most of our time in these meetings dealing with the concerns of our own congregation, and I think mission means more than that. I know there must be needs in our community that the church should be meeting, but we can't seem to find out what they are."

The Nature of Mission

In years past, if you were to say the word "mission" to a group of church members and ask what word came to mind in response, many of them would probably say, "international" or "foreign." Many of us grew up associating mission primarily with efforts to carry the gospel to other lands. Missionaries were seen as saintly souls who packed up family and belongings and went to India or China. Even the term "home mission" usually referred to efforts in places far removed from where we were. For many people, being involved in mission meant giving to the yearly offering to support the church's work overseas.

Today however, that understanding of mission is being changed. And that is as it should be! A careful reading of the Bible gives a different understanding of the church's mission. Over and over again the Scriptures point out that God's people are chosen, not simply for their own benefit, but that they might be instruments of blessing to the world. God promised Abraham that "by you all the families of the earth shall bless themselves" (Gen.12:3). In Isaiah 49:6 the Lord says:

> "It is too light a thing that you should be my servant
>   to raise up the tribes of Jacob
>   and to restore the preserved of Israel;
> I will give you as a light to the nations,
>   that my salvation may reach to the end of the earth."

First Peter 2:9 states: "You are a chosen race, a royal priesthood, a holy nation, God's own people." Why? So "that you may declare the wonderful deeds of him who called you out of darkness into his marvelous light." Shortly before he died, Jesus prayed for his chosen ones and said, "As thou didst send me into the world, so I have sent them into the world" (John 17:18). According to Matthew's Gospel, Jesus' last words before ascending into heaven were "Go therefore and make disciples of all nations" (Matt. 28:19). As the *Book of Order* puts it:

The mission of God in Christ gives shape and substance to the life and work of the Church. In Christ, the church participates in God's mission for the transformation of creation and humanity by proclaiming to all people the good news of God's love, offering all people the grace of God at font and table, and calling all people to discipleship in Christ. [F-1.01]

Mission is not a facet of the church's work or an appendage of the church. It is not a function to be carried out by special individuals alone. Neither is mission primarily something that takes place in distant lands. Instead, the church's mission is carried out when, as a body and as individuals, it seeks to know and do the will of God in its own community as well as throughout the world. This is why the church exists.

The Bible clearly teaches that from the beginning God has been working to bring about the salvation of all creation. This mission of God is the pattern for the church's mission. The 2009-2011 *Book of Order* [G-3.0101–.0103] gives us a concise review of this "salvation history":

Even when the human race broke community with its Maker and with one another, God did not forsake it, but out of grace chose one family for the sake of all, to be pilgrims of promise, God's own Israel.

God liberated the people of Israel from oppression; God covenanted with Israel to be their God and they to be God's people, that they might do justice, love mercy, and walk humbly with the Lord. . . .

God was incarnate in Jesus Christ, who announced good news to the poor, proclaimed release for prisoners and recovery of sight for the blind, let the broken victims go free, and proclaimed the year of the Lord's favor. Jesus came to seek and to save the lost; in his life and death for others God's redeeming love for all people was made visible; and in the resurrection of Jesus Christ there is the assurance of God's victory over sin and death. . . .

God's redeeming and reconciling activity in the world continues through the presence and power of the Holy Spirit, who confronts individuals and societies with Christ's Lordship of life and calls them to repentance and to obedience to the will of God.

It is in imitating Jesus by seeking and obeying God's will that the church finds its identity. It could be said that the church is most truly itself when it is engaged in mission. This is not to deny the importance of other aspects of a congregation's life, such as worship or fellowship. Rather, a church that is busy reaching out to the world will generally find its worship enhanced and its fellowship strengthened. An introverted, self-centered congregation falls short of Christ's intention for the church and cannot long prosper. Mission is the "salt" that keeps faith from becoming rancid.

Facets of the Church's Mission

What does mission look like? The answers to that question are as numerous as the shades of color in a rainbow. Each individual Christian and each congregation should be involved in mission in ways that are appropriate to their particular situation. Yet, in spite of this variety of forms, it is possible to group most of the ways we carry out our mission under one of the following three categories.

Evangelism. Evangelism has acquired a bad reputation among many Presbyterians. Perhaps the main reason for this is that we often confuse evangelism itself with certain methods of doing evangelism that make us uncomfortable. In the first example at the beginning of the chapter, Sam Washington's negative reaction to the word "evangelism" illustrates this problem.

Evangelism could be defined simply as sharing the good news. Objectively, this means telling the story of Jesus Christ and inviting those who do not know him as Savior and Lord into relationship with him. Subjectively, it means the personal witness of an individual or congregation to what God through Jesus Christ has done for them. Evangelism is so central to the mission of the church that the first of the Great Ends of the Church is "the proclamation of the gospel for the salvation of humankind" [F-1.0304].

To do evangelism does not necessarily mean that we must preach on street corners. Rather, whenever and however we share this good news with those who do not yet have a personal relationship with Christ we are involved in evangelism. This may take the form of teaching our children the truths of the faith and leading them to trust and love God. It may take the form of witnessing to those outside the faith about what the relationship with Jesus Christ has meant to us and inviting them to accept him into their lives. It may take the form of leading those who are Christian in name only (even though they may be church members) to examine their assumptions about the faith and come into a living relationship with Jesus. Evangelism may also be facilitated as new congregations are established and constituted within the larger church.

Sharing the good news is the unique mission of the church. Secular organizations may engage in activities that resemble some other facets of the church's mission, but evangelism is the responsibility of the church alone. We are the ones who have firsthand experience of what it means to know Christ as Lord and Savior; it is our duty and our privilege to share our faith with others. Sharing the good news is the ultimate goal of all the church's work. The particular programs churches develop in this area will differ, shaped by the circumstances and needs of the people around them. However, when we train people to share their faith we should be careful that the methods we use to share the gospel are consistent with the good news itself. Sessions should regularly evaluate the means by which this part of the church's mission is being carried out to make sure that they are appropriate and effective and that they have biblical and theological integrity.

In evaluating a plan or approach to evangelism, a session should satisfy itself that the plan does the following:

1. *It takes sin seriously.* Human need is a great motivating factor for sharing the good news. There are people everywhere in extreme distress. We believe that the root cause of much of this distress is alienation from God, our Creator. Self-help, psychological adjustment, or a better economic condition will not ultimately satisfy the deepest of human needs and are not the final aim of evangelism. Rather, this outreach begins with the assumption that human beings are "without hope except in God's sovereign mercy,"[1] and it seeks to restore the loving, mutual relationship with God that brings true peace and fulfillment. The deepest needs of human beings are spiritual.

2. *It focuses on Jesus Christ and God's grace.* Christian evangelism seeks to introduce people to God as revealed in Jesus Christ. For us, to know God fully means to know Jesus, and to know Jesus is to know a God of grace

and love. This is the good news: "God so loved the world that he gave his only Son, that whoever believes in him should not perish but have eternal life" (John 3:16). The object of evangelism is to introduce people to a risen, living Christ who brings healing, forgiveness, and hope into their lives. Intellectual assent to the truths of the gospel are involved in this process, but the true goal is a personal relationship of trust and commitment.

3. *It offers a new quality of life.* To be in relationship with Christ is to be a new person. The gospel promises that as we seek to follow Christ, those things that have twisted our lives and separated us from God and other people will die away. We will not be enslaved by them any longer. We will be transformed into the people we were created to be. This process takes a lifetime, and it is only possible as we live daily with Christ and claim the power of the Holy Spirit. We find support and companionship for this new life in the church. It is appropriate, as persons consider a commitment to Christ, to make them aware that this includes a call to involvement in mission. Evangelism that has integrity will seek to integrate new converts into a community of believers and to challenge them to live out their faith in the world.

4. *It respects the right to choose.* The saving relationship with God through Jesus Christ is one of freedom, love, and trust. It is not a relationship that can be coerced by means of fear or guilt. All approaches to evangelism should respect the integrity of others, especially their right to accept or reject the gospel freely. The development of faith may be a very slow process. A person may say "no" to God many times before finally saying "yes."

While presenting the gospel clearly and offering persons the opportunity to choose Christ, evangelists must be careful not to rush people into decisions they are not ready to make. Emotional manipulation works against the Holy Spirit, who is trying to enable persons to make the choice for God of their own free will. This free choice, enabled by the grace of God, is at the heart of the kind of relationship God wants to have with human beings.

Proclaiming the gospel is at the very center of all the church's work. We are called to make the good news visible in the world by our love and care for others and to make it audible through our testimony about and proclamation of God's mighty works of grace.

Service. Jesus used the image of the suffering servant from the book of Isaiah to describe his work in the world. The Gospels are full of stories reflecting Jesus' willingness to be involved in the lives of people in need. He healed the sick, cast out demons, fed the hungry, saved those terrified by storms, and raised the dead. These stories tell us that Jesus cared deeply about people, and they call us to imitate him in giving of ourselves to others.

Ministries of service should be grounded not only in compassion but also in a godly concern for justice. The biblical call to justice leads us toward the goal of "meeting the basic needs of all for food, shelter, clothing, work, health and education, in our nation and beyond. It includes justice in the context of governmental and political life, justice amidst competing economic systems and widely disparate economic conditions, and justice in racial relationships" ("The Life and Mission Statement of the Presbyterian Church (U.S.A.)," 1985, par. 27.446). This concern for justice should not be satisfied with simply meeting the needs of the moment but should drive us to grapple with the injustices that may have caused the needs.

No church can claim to be carrying out the mission to which Christ calls it unless it is involved in ministering to people outside its fellowship. These ministries will take different forms, depending on the opportunities and resources available. One church, for instance, might begin a support group for recently bereaved people in the community. Another congregation might serve a hot meal to people who otherwise would have nothing to eat. A church with a number of health-care professionals among its members might start a clinic. Another might sponsor a day-care center with scholarships for children whose parents cannot pay full tuition. A small congregation might begin a program of visitation to homebound persons in its community. A large church could begin a school for children with developmental disorders. The possibilities are as varied as the needs of people.

Ministries of compassion flow from our experience of being ministered to by a loving God. They are empowered by the Spirit of Christ dwelling in us. The first step toward a ministry of service is to be aware of what is going on in the community around the church. What are the needs of people? Helpful guidance and advice in this area can come from welfare agencies, school principals, public health officials, visiting nurses, community leaders, mental health workers, and others in the helping professions. Is there some need that no secular agency or other church is meeting?

Often the impetus to begin such a ministry will come from an individual who has had personal contact with someone in need. A news story might spur concern and lead church members to respond. Sometimes people come to the church asking for help. At other times social agencies may refer clients to the church for assistance with their problems. Every community has people who need help in some way. It is the church's task to seek them out and minister to them in the name of Christ.

The Form of Government indicates that the session may delegate the administration of programs of service to the deacons. This is particularly appropriate because it is the duty of deacons to share "in the redeeming love of Jesus Christ for the poor, the hungry, the sick, the lost, the friendless, the oppressed, and those burdened by unjust policies and structures, or anyone in distress" [G-2.0201].

It has been said that we live today in a global village.[2] The truth of this statement is borne out by the frequency with which we have the needs of people very far away from us brought into our homes by the media. As residents of this global village, we cannot claim to have fulfilled our mission of service until we have reached out beyond our local community. It is the responsibility of the session to reach into the community and the world with the message of salvation and the invitation to enter into committed discipleship [G-3.0201a]. Church members should be encouraged to participate in the mission of worldwide service through giving to general mission budgets and special offerings. It is the responsibility of the session to inform the congregation of the need for these funds and to find creative ways to motivate people to give.

Just giving money is not enough, however. Christians should be encouraged to give of themselves to people in need in and outside their own community. Our denomination, and other organizations, provide opportunities for this kind of hands-on service and ministry of presence. Congregations should also be urged to remember our denomination's mission coworkers in their prayers, not forgetting to pray for our partner churches in mission all over the world. The vocation to be a long-term mission coworker should also be held before the congregation in ways that would encourage openness to God's call.

Prophetic Witness. As the prophets of old sought to speak the word of God to the issues of their day, so must we speak God's word to the issues and evils that confront us. A third facet of our mission as disciples of Jesus is to bring the judgment and gospel of God to bear on the structures, values, and culture of our time.

As Christians become involved in ministries of service, it is natural that they should also become concerned about the causes of the problems they are seeking to remedy. Feeding hungry people may lead a congregation to grapple with the problem of unemployment, and then with deeper economic issues. A ministry with refugees might raise interest in matters of international economics or foreign policy.

Yet this movement from the particular problems to larger issues frequently raises questions about the church's right to speak on so-called secular matters. These things are often controversial and may spark conflict in the church when members have differing opinions. In spite of all this, we cannot claim to be faithful in God's mission if we are not faithful in the public arena. The Lordship of Christ extends not only to individuals but also to societies.

The mission of prophetic witness is carried out both outside and inside the church. Outside the church, we are to be involved in the reformation of the world. The gospel has a forward thrust, and it carries the whole world toward the final coming of God's reign. If Jesus is Lord of all the earth, and not just of the church, then it is appropriate that we share with him in establishing his "just, loving, and peaceable rule in the world [F-1.0302d]. This task immediately brings us into contact with social and political structures. It often involves defending these structures when good ones are threatened or, when they are contrary to God's Word, working for change and speaking out against what we believe to be wrong in them.

It is for this reason that church councils make pronouncements and write study papers on issues such as economic justice. Our pronouncements are verbal witnesses to God's claim on society. They seek to proclaim Christian values and bring these values to bear on particular issues. They are guides to church members in the ethical decisions of life. They are announcements to those outside the church of what we believe God's word to be on a certain issue.

Changing structures, whether on the local, national, or world level, is a difficult task. It is usually accomplished most effectively as congregations, councils, and ecumenical groups join together in common witness, prayer, and action.

One particular area of prophetic witness that has come to the fore in recent years is that of peacemaking. We believe that Christians are called to seek the good of all people, not just our own good. "The world is torn and divided by hostility, suspicion and the oppressive use of power and resources. Peace can only be achieved on the basis of just and sustaining relationships among all people" ("The Life and Mission Statement of the Presbyterian Church (U.S.A.)," 1985, par. 27.448). The future of our world may depend on how faithful Christians are in this area of our witness. "We continue to seek peace not in fear but with hope, through Christ who breaks through every barrier of division and hostility to be our peace and the world's" ("Life and Mission Statement," 1985, par. 27.448). It is the duty of all Christians to do what they can as individuals to make a difference for good in the world. The great problems of our day—hunger, war, racism, poverty, and the threat of terrorism, among others—may seem insurmountable. Yet apathy and discouragement indicate lack of faith in the God for whom all things are possible.

The reformation of the world and its values to bring them more into line with the intentions of God is not a task we undertake or expect to accomplish by human effort alone. The Holy Spirit of Christ must guide and empower us or the work will be doomed from the start. So it is that "the Church worships and serves, with confidence that God's rule has been established and with firm hope in the ultimate manifestation of the triumph of God" [W-7.6001].

A second area of prophetic witness is the reformation of the church itself. In the Christian community we are to live out the promises of God so that those outside the church can see a picture of what God is doing in the world. This does not mean that the church is perfect; in fact, most sins found in the world can be found in the church. Rather we are to be engaged in a continual process of self-examination, confession, and renewal. The motto "always being reformed" is a Presbyterian witness to God's grace and power, as well as a confession of human imperfection. We should never be content to tolerate in the church the sins that we deplore in the world—pride, corruption, immorality, injustice, and prejudice. Rather we are always to be working to make the whole life of the church into a witness for God.

It is the responsibility of the session of a particular church to lead the church in self-examination, "warning and bearing witness against error in doctrine and immorality in practice within the congregation" [G-3.0201c]. The session itself should always be alert to opportunities for the church to be more Christ-like. Every area of the church's life should reflect the goodness and justice of God. In order for this mission of the reformation of the church to be carried out, the *Book of Order* [F-1.0404] states that

As it participates in God's mission, the Presbyterian Church (U.S.A.) seeks:

a new openness to the sovereign activity of God in the Church and in the world, to a more radical obedience to Christ, and to a more joyous celebration in worship and work;

a new openness in its own membership, becoming in fact as well as in faith a community of women and men of all ages, races, ethnicities, and worldly conditions, made one in Christ by the power of the Spirit, as a visible sign of the new humanity;

a new openness to see both the possibilities and perils of its institutional forms in order to ensure the faithfulness and usefulness of these forms to God's activity in the world; and

a new openness to God's continuing reformation of the Church ecumenical, that it might be more effective in its mission.

By keeping itself alert and open to the movement of the Holy Spirit, the church can allow God to reform it until it is more nearly the image of Christ in the world. Then the very life of the church itself will be a witness to the good news.

Beyond Polity

Much of the work of the session is involved in leading the church in mission. It is a complex and often difficult responsibility. Effective mission seldom simply happens. It requires careful discernment, much prayer, as well as efficient planning, administration, and evaluation. The focus of this book is polity, and the actual process by which a session plans and carries out mission is beyond its scope. However, session members who are concerned with leading this area of the church's life should make a careful study of the ways in which a church can be equipped and guided by the Spirit of God for their congregation's unique calling.

An Ecumenical Note

The mission that Jesus Christ entrusted to his church is greater than any one denomination or religious body. It calls all Christians to put their differences aside in order to find common ministries in the world. This century has seen the growth of tolerance and unity among believers of different communions. In working together in common ministries, we have found that we indeed have "one Lord, one faith, one baptism, one God and Father of us all" (Eph. 4:5–6). While questions of doctrine and practice may still separate us, we sense the reality of each other's faith when we serve soup together at a night shelter or work together to sponsor refugee families. Cooperation across ecumenical lines allows the combining of resources and talents. This helps us to accomplish together more than one church could accomplish alone.

Christian unity is also an important tool for witness and evangelism. Jesus himself prayed that his followers might be united "so that the world may know that thou hast sent me and hast loved them even as thou hast loved me" (John 17:23). When the church of Jesus Christ speaks with a unified voice, the world is more likely to listen. Also our unity is a sign to the world of the peace and power of God.

On the subject of ecumenical relations and mission, the *Book of Order* [G-5.0101] states:

> The Presbyterian Church (U.S.A.) at all levels seeks to manifest more visibly the unity of the body of Christ and will be open to opportunities for conversation, cooperation, and action with other ecclesiastical groups.

This means that sessions, presbyteries, and higher councils should always be alert to ways they can join in mission with other Christian churches.

Mission is the heartbeat of the church. We are called to be faithful disciples of our Lord, who spent his life sharing the good news, serving others, and witnessing to God's love and purpose for the world. This task may not always be easy or comfortable. However, in spite of the difficulties the Church is called to be a community of faith, hope, love, and witness "even at the risk of losing its life" [F-1.0301].

Questions for Reflection and Discussion

1. When you hear the word "mission" at church, what comes to your mind?

2. Have you ever been involved in a mission activity that took you off the property of your church? Is so, what did you enjoy about it? Did anything make you uncomfortable? Would you do it again? Why?

3. What percentage of the money your church receives goes toward mission outside the congregation? Is that proportion acceptable?

4. Can a person's job be his or her mission? Have you ever felt this way about your own work?

Chapter Ten

PRESBYTERY, SYNOD, AND THE GENERAL ASSEMBLY

Paul Allan and his pastor were on their way to attend a meeting of presbytery. Paul noticed a large book titled "Minutes" on the back seat of the car and asked what it was. His pastor explained that these were the minutes of the meetings of their session during the past year and that he was taking them to the presbytery meeting to be reviewed. "Do they think we are doing something wrong?" asked Paul. "Why does presbytery want to review our minutes?"

Sally Coe was attending a new-member class, and the subject for the evening was the way that presbytery, synod, and the General Assembly function. After the pastor's presentation, Sally commented, "I think I know something about what presbyteries do because I served on my presbytery's youth council when I was a teenager. And I believe I understand the basics about the General Assembly and its work. But I don't understand how synods fit into the picture at all."

The session of Highdale Presbyterian Church was studying the sacraments together as part of their annual continuing education retreat. The topic of children receiving Communion arose, and one ruling elder questioned whether it was really necessary for children to be baptized before participating in the sacrament. "In spite of what the *Book of Order* says, it doesn't seem right to me that children should be denied the Lord's Supper because their parents have not had them baptized. I wish I knew how to try to get this rule changed."

More-Inclusive Councils

Individual teaching elders and ruling elders have no power of governance in the Presbyterian system of polity. Their authority is always exercised in groups of presbyters constituted as councils. These councils represent the unity of the church beyond the level of the particular congregation.

At some time in their careers, most ruling elders will have the opportunity to serve as commissioners to a council beyond the session. Indeed, it is the duty of both ruling elders and teaching elders to serve not only their particular congregation but also the church at large [G-2.0301]. When elected to serve as members of presbytery, synod, or the General Assembly, "ruling elders participate and vote with the same authority as teaching elders of the Word and Sacrament, and they are eligible for any office" [G-2.0301]. The Form of Government specifies that higher councils are made up of equal numbers of teaching elders and ruling elders. This helps to ensure that a true parity will exist between the two kinds of presbyters and that the members who are teaching elders will not consistently outnumber those who are ruling elders.

The councils now in use that are more inclusive than the session in the Presbyterian Church (U.S.A.) are presbytery, synod, and the General Assembly. They are constituted in ascending order, that is, presbytery exercises governance over a number of sessions, synod over a number of presbyteries, and the General Assembly over the whole church. In regard to the relationships between councils, the *Book of Order* [G-3.0101] states that

The mutual interconnection of the church through its councils is a sign of the unity of the church. Congregations of the Presbyterian Church (U.S.A.), while possessing all the gifts necessary to be the church, are nonetheless not sufficient in themselves to be the church. Rather, they are called to share with others both within and beyond the congregation the task of bearing witness to the Lordship of Jesus Christ in the world.

Further in F-3.0206 we read: "A higher council shall have the right of review and control over a lower one and shall have the power to determine matters of controversy upon reference, complaint, or appeal."

One application of the above principles is that each more-inclusive council reviews the minutes of meetings of the bodies it oversees. In answer to the question raised in the first example at the beginning of the chapter, presbytery's request to see the minutes of a session is generally not due to any suspicion of wrongdoing. This is a regular procedure required by the Constitution [G-3.0101]. Reviewing minutes is one way that a council exercises its responsibility to review the actions of the councils for which it is responsible. If the reviewing body does happen to find significant error in the proceedings, it can require that the error be corrected.

As stated above, councils have only those powers specifically granted to them by the Constitution. This principle, along with that of the relationships among councils, is important in understanding how presbytery, synod, and the General Assembly work together. These aspects of our polity can be reviewed in chapter 1 of this book. Rules relating to the meetings of councils are discussed in chapter 12.

Responsibilities in Common. All councils of the church (including the session) have certain responsibilities in common. They "do those things necessary to the peace, purity, unity, and progress of the church under the will of Christ" [G-3.0102]. Any and all powers exercised by councils are strictly within the bounds of the church and have no force of civil law. The councils of the church "exist to help congregations and the church as a whole to be more faithful participants in the mission of Christ" [G-3.0101]. Most of the duties of presbytery, synod, and the General Assembly, as well as those of the session, are under three headings. According to G-3.0101 they are to:

> provide that the Word of God may be truly preached and
> heard,
> provide that the Sacraments may be rightly administered
> and received, and
> nurture the covenant community of disciples of Christ.

The following is a brief review of some specific areas involved in carrying forth this work. As councils do these things, the Form of Government instructs them to be guided by "the marks of the Church" (F-1.0302), the notes by which Presbyterian and Reformed communities have identified themselves through history (F-1.0303) and the six Great Ends of the Church (F-1.0304)" [G-3.0501].

1. *Missional leadership, guidance, and nurture.* This responsibility involves helping the councils they oversee to excel in carrying out the mission of God. This responsibility may include, among other things, resourcing for mission, promoting awareness of needs in the world, training persons to engage in mission, and establishing productive mission partnership between our congregations and those of partner churches.

2. *Providing for the Word of God to be preached and the Sacraments administered.* This function covers everything from the preparation of Communion at the congregational level to the preparation of candidates for ministry at the presbytery and General Assembly levels.

3. *Nurture the covenant community of disciples of Christ.* This shared responsibility has to do with cultivating communication and helpful relationships between congregations and councils and protecting the ties that bind us together in the body of Christ, both denominationally and ecumenically. Paying attention to the principles of unity in diversity stated in F-1.0403 is also included under this heading. "Each council shall develop procedures and mechanisms for promoting and reviewing that body's implementation of the church's commitment to inclusiveness and representation" [G-3.0103]. It is required that each council above the session have a committee on representation that will advise the council in this work.

4. *Judicial functions.* Presbytery, synod, and the General Assembly are each given the responsibility to "serve in judicial matters in accordance with the Rules of Discipline" [G-3.0109a]. These responsibilities are generally carried out through permanent judicial commissions and are discussed more fully in chapter 13 of this book.

5. *Review and control.* As discussed above, each council is to review regularly the activities of the councils over which it has jurisdiction to make sure that they are in accord with the Constitution of the church. This is generally done by reviewing the minutes of meetings. This function of review and control is discussed more fully in chapter 1 of this book.

6. *Ecumenical relations.* At its own level each presbytery and synod and the General Assembly are to "seek to manifest more visibly the unity of the body of Christ and . . . be open to opportunities for conversation, cooperation, and action with other ecclesiastical groups" [G-5.0101]. This ordinarily means that each council relates to some comparable council of another Christian church or participates in councils of churches in its area of jurisdiction.

7. *Administration.* Each more-inclusive council has the responsibility and is given the power to set up any work groups, committees, commissions, etc., required to help it do its work. The current Form of Government leaves a great deal of flexibility for councils to create those structures. However, they should be formed around the particular mission the council is called to carry out. Each council is required to develop its own administrative manual that will form and guide its mission work.

8. *Warning against error.* The *Book of Order* states that the duty and powers of councils include "warning and bearing witness against error in doctrine and immorality in practice," in its area of jurisdiction [G-3.0201c; 3.0301c; 3.0401c; 3.0501c]. This power relates to the church's mission of prophetic witness as well as to the ministry of discipline and pastoral care.

9. *Committee on representation.* Each council above the session level is required to form a committee on representation as described in G-3.0103. This group has the responsibility to advise the church as to how well the council's life implements the principles of unity in diversity [F-1.0403].

10. *Adopting and implementing a sexual misconduct policy.* Each council, including the session, is required to have such a policy and put it into action for the safety of those in their care [G-3.0106].

11. *Budgeting and per capita.* Funding the administrative operating expenses of councils above the session is done through the collecting of per capita payments from constituent churches. Presbyteries are to raise their own funding and also to raise and transmit per capita funds to the synod and presbytery. This transmission shall be done in a timely fashion [G-3.0106].

The remainder of this chapter will give a brief survey of the responsibilities and powers peculiar to each of the three more-inclusive councils and then of the administrative structures that all more-inclusive councils may use to carry out their work. It is not intended as an exhaustive explanation of all the duties of presbytery, synod, and the General Assembly. Anyone who is elected a commissioner to one of these councils should make a careful study of the appropriate sections of the *Book of Order* and of the manual of the council on which he or she will serve.

Presbytery

The linchpin of the Presbyterian system of church government—the presbytery—originated in Scotland in the sixteenth century. It was devised in order to bind local congregations scattered across the nation into one denomination while protecting the freedom of those congregations to elect their own leaders. Without resorting to the use of the unpalatable (to Presbyterians) office of bishop, presbyteries provided the administrative machinery necessary for "efficient central and local organization on a national scale."[1] In fact, it can be argued that the presbytery serves basically the same function in Presbyterian polity that the bishop serves in episcopal polity.

Presbytery is the council next above the session, and it has jurisdiction over the sessions of all Presbyterian Church (U.S.A.) congregations within its geographical bounds. A presbytery is composed of all the congregations and teaching elders within that district [G-3.0301]. Since the goal is to have equal numbers of ruling and teaching elders at a presbytery meeting, each presbytery must adopt and communicate to the sessions within it bounds "a plan for determining how many ruling elders each session should elect as commissioners to presbytery" [G-3.0301]. When the presbytery meets for business, its members include all teaching elders who have been received into the presbytery, all elders properly commissioned by their sessions to represent the congregations at that meeting, and any elders from churches selected by presbytery to redress any imbalance between the numbers of teaching elders and ruling elders. Officers of the presbytery who are ruling elders are automatically members of presbytery during their term of office. Presbytery may also decide if and how ruling elders serving as moderators of commissions and committees of the presbytery may be voting members of presbytery.

The Responsibilities of Presbytery. The work that is peculiar to the presbytery falls into three general categories: that relating to congregations; that relating to teaching elders, those preparing for this ministry, and certain others serving the church; and that relating to synod and the General Assembly. Presbytery's responsibilities are detailed in G-3.03.

1. *Relating to congregations.* Presbytery is responsible for a wide range of duties and powers in relation to its congregations. In addition to those mentioned above in the discussion of common duties, the presbytery is to

> provide help to congregations in the areas of mission, including prophetic witness, worship, evangelism, leadership development, and administration; presbytery is responsible to develop a coordinated strategy for mission in its bounds;
>
> organize new congregations, merge or divide congregations, and dismiss congregations to another denomination or dissolve the congregation, all this being done in consultation with the church's members;
>
> oversee congregations without pastors and give special attention to their needs;
>
> establish and dissolve pastoral relationships;
>
> encourage ecumenical relationships that enhance the life and mission of the church;
>
> authorize the Lord's Supper for fellowship and other groups that do not have sessions;
>
> train ruling elders to administer the Lord's Supper when needed;
>
> give pastoral care to congregations;
>
> commission ruling elders for pastoral service when needed;
>
> counsel, resource, and/or mediate with a session reporting difficulties to the end of promoting peace and unity;
>
> provide stewardship education;
>
> decide where new churches will be located or where an existing congregation may move;
>
> consider and act on requests from congregations to take the actions regarding real property as described in G-4.0206;
>
> appoint administrative commissions to act in the place of sessions when necessary. (See G-3.03.)

It is wise for sessions to be visited by representatives of the presbytery on a regular basis. These visits provide an opportunity for concerns and needs of the session to be voiced to the representatives of presbytery, making for improved communication and care between the councils. Presbytery's representatives can also lift up the work of presbytery and the wider church.

2. *Relating to teaching elders, those in preparation to be teaching elders, and to those in certified church service.* A significant amount of work allotted to the presbytery in the *Book of Order* deals with matters relating to church professionals and those preparing to be so. Ordinarily each teaching elder is a member of the presbytery where he or she works. Presbytery is to function as the pastor and counselor of its teaching elders, along with commissioned ruling elders to particular pastoral service and certified Christian educators [G-3.0307]. This pastoral function is an important one and should be taken seriously, particularly in light of the fact that many teaching elders, commissioned ruling elders, and educators have no other source of pastoral care. It is up to the presbytery to decide what structures are needed to fulfill this duty with excellence and consistency.

Presbytery has the power to ordain, receive, dismiss, install, remove, and discipline teaching elders [G-3.0301c]. This means that congregations do not have absolute power over the hiring and firing of teaching elders. A church has no ability to dissolve the pastoral relationship on its own. Instead, it makes a request to presbytery that this be done, and if the request is in order and in the best interest of the church, presbytery may grant the request.

Not all teaching elders are pastors of particular churches. Presbytery also has responsibility for oversight of those teaching elders who work in other settings. Therefore it has the power to "designate teaching elders to work as teachers, evangelists, administrators, chaplains, and in other forms of ministry recognized as appropriate by the presbytery" [G-3.0306]. These teaching elders have the same rights in and responsibilities toward presbytery as those who are pastors.

In addition to its relationships with teaching elders, presbytery is also responsible to care for inquirers and candidates for the ministry. The *Book of Order* specifies that "a presbytery shall enter into covenant relationship with those preparing to become teaching elders and with their sessions and congregations " [G-2.0601]. The presbytery is responsible to create the administrative structures and groups needed to make sure that inquirers and candidates receive full care, oversight, and adequate preparation for their future ministry. Presbytery must provide the means to examine and certify a candidate before he or she may enter into negotiation to provide pastoral service [G-2.0607]. Presbytery may transfer candidates or inquirers to other presbyteries or remove them from the rolls of those preparing to be teaching elders [G-2.0608–.0609]. Finally, presbytery is charged to provide persons to serve as readers of ordination examinations [G-3.0302b].

Persons in certified church service have invested significant amounts of time and money to sharpen their skills and deepen their knowledge about their area of ministry. Their ranks include administrative personnel, educators, and musicians. The Form of Government requires presbytery to recognize and support their work in a number of ways. In addition, if presbytery so decides, they may receive the privilege of speaking at presbytery meetings [G-2.1102].

The ministries of Certified Christian Educators and Associate Christian Educators are specifically recognized in the *Book of Order*. The presbytery is responsible to establish minimum terms of employment, including compensation and benefits, for such persons. They are allowed direct communication with the group or person in the presbytery who oversees ministry. Also while serving in an educational setting under the jurisdiction of the presbytery, they may be given the privilege to speak at presbytery meetings. If they are ruling elders, they may also be allowed to vote [G-2.1103].

3. *Relating to synod and the General Assembly.* Another major function of presbytery is relating to the two more-inclusive councils [G-3.0302]. This is a very important function in that crucial communications between the more-inclusive councils and sessions of local churches are often funneled through the presbytery. Presbytery participates in the deliberations of synod and of the General Assembly by electing commissioners to serve as members of these councils at a particular meeting or meetings. It also hears and receives reports from the commissioners when they return from the meetings. Further, the *Book of Order* specifies that the presbytery is responsible for ensuring that the orders of the more-inclusive councils are carried out within the presbytery.

Presbytery has the privilege and the duty to propose to the synod or the General Assembly "such measures as may be of common concern to the mission of the church" [G-3.0302d]. This is an avenue of change in the church. For instance, in the example at the beginning of the chapter, the ruling elder concerned about unbaptized children could have used this avenue to get his concern before the wider church. He could have written what is called an "overture," expressing his thoughts on the matter and suggesting a particular remedy. This overture could be presented to his session and, if adopted, could be sent to the presbytery for its adoption. The overture could be discussed at a meeting of presbytery, and, if adopted by presbytery, it would be sent to the General Assembly for action. Presbytery can also originate overtures itself when necessary, and overtures relating to regional concerns may be sent to synod for action. For example, a presbytery might originate an overture to synod asking that a nursing home be built within the bounds of the synod.

A particularly important function in this area is that of amending the Constitution of the church. This is a matter in which the presbyteries and the General Assembly work together. When an amendment to the *Book of Order* is properly proposed (often through overtures from presbyteries) and approved by one General Assembly, it is sent out to all the presbyteries of the church for their affirmative or negative vote. Affirmative votes by a simple majority of the presbyteries are required to amend the *Book of Order*. If the required number of presbyteries vote in the affirmative, the change is enacted one year from the adjournment of the Assembly that sent it to the presbyteries. All such amendments must be voted on as they stand by the presbyteries. They cannot be amended or changed in any way. If the necessary majority vote by the presbyteries is not achieved, the suggested amendment fails. These processes for amendment are detailed in G-6.04.

Amending the *Book of Confessions* requires a different procedure and a higher proportion of presbyteries to approve. If the proposal to amend the *Book of Confessions* passes at a meeting of the General Assembly, it is then sent to a committee appointed to study the matter. The report of this committee goes to the next General Assembly for vote. If it passes then it is sent to the presbyteries for their vote. Such a change to the *Book of Confessions* must have a two-thirds affirmative vote to be enacted. If the amendment receives the two-thirds vote for approval, then it is approved and enacted by the next General Assembly. Section 6.03 of the Form of Government contains more detailed provisions for these changes.

Synod

The council next above the presbytery is synod. Over seventy years before the first meeting of a Presbyterian General Assembly in this country, the first synod was already in operation. It was organized as the Synod of Philadelphia in 1717, with four member presbyteries.

Synods are regional in nature, providing a broader base for mission than is usually available to individual presbyteries. Depending on a number of factors, including density of population and the number of churches in a given region, the geographical bounds of synods will vary. However, each synod must be composed of not fewer than three presbyteries [G-3.0401]. When the synod meets for business, its members are those commissioners (both ruling elders and teaching elders) elected by the constituent presbyteries.

The Responsibilities of Synod. The two main thrusts of synod's ministry involve relationship with its presbyteries and its work related to the General Assembly.

1. *Relating to its presbyteries.* The responsibility of synod to its member presbyteries is broadly analogous to the responsibility presbytery has for its constituent congregations. In addition to the duties of synod toward presbyteries discussed under the heading "Responsibilities in Common," on page 86, the *Book of Order* cites a number of others. One of the most important functions of synod is described in G-3.0401a. The section relating to providing that the Word of God is truly preached and heard says that the synod

may develop with its presbyteries "a broad strategy of mission for the mission of the church within its bounds and in accord with the larger strategy of the General Assembly."

It is often more efficient and better stewardship for synod to do or provide certain things for all its presbyteries than for each presbytery to duplicate the effort. In some cases, synod enables ministries that would be difficult or impossible for a single presbytery to support. For instance, synod may provide resources to support new church development among its presbyteries jointly or singly. Or, while there may be only a handful of people in a single presbytery interested in the problems of drug and alcohol abuse, synod could provide training and planning opportunities in this area for all its presbyteries. In this way synod helps to broaden the quality of programs and the scope of mission of its member presbyteries [G-3.0401a].

Synods also help the presbyteries as needed to develop plans and find resources for their own mission [G-3.0403a, b, c]. It works with the presbyteries to assist in the matters related to calling teaching elders as needed. The mission of synod to its presbyteries is summed up by the Form of Government saying that synod is responsible for "providing such services of education and nurture as it presbyteries may require; providing encouragement, guidance, resources to presbyteries in the areas of mission, prophetic witness, leadership development, worship, evangelism, and responsible administration" [G-3.0401c].

Administratively, synod reviews the minutes of its presbyteries regularly to exercise review and control. It is to broaden communication within the synod between presbyteries and with the General Assembly. Furthering ecumenical relationship within it boundaries is also one of synod's duties. Added to these functions, the permanent judicial commissions of synod are an important part of the judicial system of our church.

The *Book of Order* also lists several powers that synods have in relation to presbyteries. Along with those common powers discussed earlier, synod shapes the boundaries of presbyteries within its area. Included is the power of "organizing new presbyteries, dividing, uniting, or otherwise combining presbyteries or portions of presbyteries previously existing" [G-3.0403c]. Synods may also take action, subject to the General Assembly, to form within its bounds new presbyteries that further the mission of racial ethnic or immigrant congregations.

2. *Relating to the General Assembly.* The responsibilities of synod in relationship to the General Assembly are more limited than those of presbyteries. Synods do not, for example, elect commissioners to the General Assembly; this right is reserved for presbyteries. Synods are charged, however, with seeing that the actions and orders of the General Assembly are communicated and carried out within the synod.

Synods, like presbyteries, are also responsible for proposing to the

General Assembly "such measures as may be of common concern to the mission of the whole Church" [G-3.0402]. This responsibility reflects the other side of communication between the presbyteries and the General Assembly. Not only does synod tell the presbyteries what the General Assembly has decided, but it also communicates to the General Assembly the concerns of the presbyteries.

The Form of Government [G-3.0404] contains a provision that allows a synod to reduce the work it does to two functions. These are the minimum: exercising administrative review over its presbyteries and serving in judicial process as noted in the Rules of Discipline. It takes a two-thirds majority of the constituent presbyteries to choose this option. If a synod does reduce its functions in this way, the work it chooses not to do is taken by the presbyteries upon mutual agreement

As of the writing of this book a task force appointed by the General Assembly is at work studying possible changes to the middle governing bodies of the church. It is possible that they may propose radical changes in the form of synods or even eliminate them entirely. If synods are eliminated, their most important functions will be carried on in some fashion within the governing bodies of the church.

The General Assembly

The first meeting of a Presbyterian General Assembly in the United States was held in 1789 in Philadelphia, Pennsylvania. It reflected the practice of the Scottish Church in gathering commissioners from all the presbyteries to meet together and conduct business on a denomination-wide basis. The unity of the separate parts of the church—congregations, sessions, presbyteries, and synods—is represented by the General Assembly. When it meets for business, its members are the commissioners (ruling elders and teaching elders in equal numbers) elected by the presbyteries.

The Responsibilities of the General Assembly. "The General Assembly is the council of the whole church" [G-3.0501]. The powers and duties of the General Assembly are many and wide-ranging. A number of these have already been discussed in the section on common responsibilities. Here we will focus on duties and powers in two main areas: those relating specifically to presbyteries and synods and those relating to the whole church.

1. *Relating to synods.* As the most-inclusive council, the General Assembly has particular responsibilities toward the synods of the church. The General Assembly oversees the work of synods assisting them as needed to take an active, effective role in promoting the health of the church and its mission within their bounds. This includes providing resources and leadership training for those who serve as constitutional officers and members of constitutional committees in synods and presbyteries.

The General Assembly also exercises review and control over the synods, reviewing their minutes and seeing that they act in accord with the Constitution of the church. One facet of governance is that of setting the boundaries of synods. The General Assembly is responsible for "organizing new synods, or dividing, uniting, or otherwise combining synods or portions of synods previously existing" [G-3.0502d]. As mentioned above, when synods desire to change the boundaries of presbyteries or organize new presbyteries, the General Assembly must approve their proposals [G-3.0403c].

2. *Relating to the entire church.* The General Assembly "constitutes the bond of union, community, and mission among all its congregations and councils, to the end that the whole church becomes a community of faith, hope, love, and witness" [G-3.0501]. For this reason, many of the responsibilities of the General Assembly are carried out in relation to or on behalf of the whole denomination, and beyond to other faith groups.

The first duties listed in the *Book of Order* are those involved with mission and program. The General Assembly sets priorities, develops objectives and strategies, and provides resources to carry out the mission of the entire denomination. This includes programs and ministries of evangelism, service, and prophetic witness. The character of these programs should be such as will foster diversity and balance within the mission of the whole church. The General Assembly, as is true with all councils, is also authorized to set up the administrative systems needed to carry out this mission [G-3.0501a].

The sphere of mission for the General Assembly is the entire world. While other councils may engage in specific mission projects elsewhere in this country or overseas, the Assembly coordinates the overall national and international mission program of the church. The General Assembly commissions mission coworkers for their ministries. It also maintains relationships with our partner denominations in other countries and coordinates significant parts of our work with them.

Another duty is to provide "those services, resources, and programs performed most effectively at a national level" [G-3.0501c]. These services may include a denominational curriculum for the education program of the congregation, a denominational press that publishes books of particular interest to Presbyterians, and systems for coordinating the movement of teaching elders within the church. In order to fulfill its responsibility to provide for communication within the church, the General Assembly may support a denominational magazine and/or newspaper. The General Assembly also provides resources and guidance for the evangelism, justice, and service ministries of less-inclusive councils. As with presbyteries and synods, the General Assembly is allowed to form and oversee any agencies or other groups necessary to carry out this work.

On behalf of the whole church, the General Assembly maintains relationships with bodies of other Christian denominations. Representatives of these groups are often invited to meetings of the General Assembly as ecumenical participants. The Constitution also gives the General Assembly certain powers relating to receiving or uniting with other ecclesiastical bodies under the provisions of Chapter 5 of the Form of Government.

One such exercise in ecumenical relating is the "Formula of Agreement" between our church, the Evangelical Lutheran Church in America, the Reformed Church in America, and the United Church of Christ. The formula was voted by the 1997 General Assembly and approved by the presbyteries, going into effect in June 1998. This formula for full communion, along with a covenant relationship document with the Korean Presbyterian Church in America, are in the appendix section of the Form of Government. Full communion means that there is mutual recognition among the churches that each is a true church of Jesus Christ and also that each will recognize ordinations to ministry by the other churches as valid. Celebrating the Lord's Supper together is also part of full communion.

As the highest council in the church, the General Assembly is given the power to decide controversies brought before it and to give advice and instruction in cases submitted to it, in conformity with the Constitution [G-3.0501c]. In cases of judicial process, the General Assembly exercises this function through its permanent judicial commission. The rulings of this permanent judicial commission in appeals from the decisions of lower councils are final.

Often issues of concern to the wider church will be brought before the General Assembly in the form of overtures from lower councils or of resolutions from commissioners to the General Assembly. The decisions and advice of the General Assembly on these matters are printed in its minutes. From time to time in carrying out this duty the General Assembly will also authorize statements or study papers on current issues to be written and distributed to the churches. These actions come under the heading of fulfilling its duty of "communicating with the whole church on matters of common concern; warning and bearing witness against errors in doctrine or immorality in the church and in the world" [G-3.0501c].

Commissions and Committees

The *Book of Order* states that a council "may delegate aspects of its tasks to entities as it deems appropriate, provided that those entities remain accountable to the council" [G-3.0106]. The former Form of Government specified a number of specific structures that each council above the session was required to have. At the presbytery level, for example, these included the Committee on Ministry and the Committee on Preparation for Ministry.

The new Form of Government does not require these specific groups. However, it does require that presbytery fulfill the functions that these groups fulfilled under the former Constitution. It is up to each presbytery to create and name the task groups to fulfill these functions. This gives each council above the session new freedom to structure its work in ways that best allow its mission to flourish. The one committee of this sort still specifically required under the new Form of Government is the committee on representation [G-3.0103].

A commission is a group empowered to "consider and conclude matters referred to it by a council" [G-3.0109]. Disposition by a commission is final disposition, except that decisions of an administrative commission may be rescinded or changed when reported to the council that appointed it [G-3.0109b]. When actions of commissions are reported to the council and recorded in its minutes, they become the actions of the body itself. In the case of judicial commissions, the decision of the commission becomes a final judgment when a copy of the written decision is signed by the clerk and moderator of the commission [D-7.0402(c)].

There are two types of commissions: administrative and judicial. Sessions may appoint administrative commissions to deal with matters regarding new ruling elders and deacons, receiving and dismissing members, and settling differences in the congregation. The functions of administrative commissions of presbytery may include examining and receiving into membership teaching elders, approving their terms of call, ordaining and installing teaching elders, engaging in specific mission such as immigrant fellowships, working with new congregations, and forming union or federated congregation made up of churches of different denominations.

All councils above the session may form commissions to look into troubled situations in the areas of their jurisdiction. Each of the four councils may also form administrative commissions to deal with pastoral (not judicial) matters arising from sexual abuse in the church when the accused has died or renounced the jurisdiction of the church. These commissions seek truth and healing. More detailed instructions regarding administrative commissions and their use are found in G-3.0109b.

Judicial commissions consider and decide cases of process. Every presbytery and synod and the General Assembly must have a permanent judicial commission to serve as outlined in the Rules of Discipline. Matters concerning the work of these commissions are found in Chapter 13 of this book.

A committee has a narrower field of responsibility than a commission, serving only to "study and recommend action or carry out decisions already made by a council" [G-3.0109]. The recommendations of committees must be reported to their council and must be acted on before they take effect.

Much of the work of the church is carried out by committees of one sort or another. The work these bodies do is crucial to the effective functioning of the church. For instance, nominating committees propose persons to serve on elected bodies of the church at all levels and also nominate teaching elders to serve in installed positions for congregations. The Form of Government requires presbytery, synod, and the General Assembly to have some sort of entity to make nominations relating to elected positions. All these nominating committees are to carry their work forward in concert with the church's commitments to diversity [F-1.0403].

At the General Assembly level, the Advisory Committee on the Constitution counsels the General Assembly on all questions relating to the interpretation of the *Book of Order*, including proposed changes. In preparation for meetings of the General Assembly, all new business that relates to the Constitution is referred to this committee for consideration and recommendation. Their recommendations help guide commissioners in making wise decisions on matters that are sometimes very complex.

Each presbytery and synod and the General Assembly is required to have a committee on representation [G-3.0103]. The committee on representation plays such an important part in our church's quest for inclusiveness and diversity that the *Book of Order* was revised in 1998 to specify that "a committee on representation should not be merged with another committee or made a subcommittee of any other committee" [G-3.0103].

This committee acts as an advocate for persons of different age groups (youth and the elderly, for example), women, persons with disabilities, and racial ethnic group members within the structures of the council. The committee on representation is a resource for the nominating committee, suggesting names of qualified persons in these groups and working to locate such persons who are willing to serve. The committee on representation also seeks to ensure that the hiring practices of the body are in line with what our Constitution says about inclusiveness in the church. It has no power to appoint anyone to an ordered ministry or position or to require that certain quotas be filled; rather, it functions to monitor and promote inclusiveness.

The *Book of Order* allows for councils to establish the structures needed to carry out their work. These groups could include task forces, boards, agencies, and advocacy groups of various sorts.

The system of related councils that our polity provides draws Christians from far-flung locations into one denomination. Each session, presbytery, synod, and the General Assembly exercises governance over and carries out mission in the particular part of the denomination that is under its jurisdiction. The relationships between these councils enable a worldwide mission and express the essential unity of the church.

Questions for Reflection and Discussion

1. Have you ever been to a presbytery, synod, or General Assembly meeting? If so, what was your general impression? What were the most and least interesting things about the meeting? How did this experience help you to better understand the relational nature of our church?

2. Find out about your synod from your teaching elder or some other knowledgeable person. What functions does it fulfill for presbyteries? How does the work of synod touch your congregation?

3. On your computer go to www.pcusa.org. What impression do you get about the denomination from the Web site? What resources do you find there? What can you tell about the mission of the PC(USA) from the Web site?

4. How would you respond to the question, Why do we need a denomination?

Chapter Eleven

STEWARDSHIP, FINANCE, AND PROPERTY

Ruth Diaz, a newly installed ruling elder, has just attended her first session meeting. In talking with her family about it, she mentions that the agenda included a financial report and review of the church's budget, as well as a rather lengthy discussion about the stewardship campaign being planned for the fall. "I'm surprised that the session would spend all that time talking about money," comments her husband. "Aren't the trustees supposed to be responsible for that kind of thing?"

Offerings during the summer have been low at First Presbyterian Church, and there is not enough money in the church's bank account to pay the pastor's salary for July. In the course of the session meeting called to discuss this problem, one ruling elder mentions that several thousand dollars have been accumulated from special gifts toward the purchase of a new organ for the sanctuary. He suggests that this money be used temporarily to make up the shortfall in pledges. A motion to use these funds is made and seconded, but several ruling elders are troubled by the idea. What is wrong with using these special gifts to pay the pastor's salary?

Suburban Presbyterian Church has received an offer to buy five acres of its undeveloped property from a local builder who plans to put a shopping center on it. A congregational meeting is called to discuss this possibility. In the course of the meeting the pastor announces that before the congregation can sell its property, the session must obtain the written permission of presbytery. Soon afterward a member of the congregation takes the floor to ask, "This property has belonged to our congregation for a long time. We paid for it, and we hold title to it. Why do we need to have presbytery's permission to sell it?"

The Grace of Stewardship

To many people, "stewardship" is a euphemism for church fund-raising. A stewardship sermon is a sermon asking for money. Stewardship visitation is a means of obtaining pledges to underwrite the church's budget. Stewardship Sunday is the day those pledges are collected. The whole business is seen as a necessary evil inflicted on the church once a year and somehow foreign to the real meaning of Christianity.

Underlying this attitude are two common, but faulty, ideas. The first is that what we earn or own is ours absolutely, by right of labor or inheritance, to dispose of as we see fit. The second is that money, being secular, is alien to the spiritual character of the church, an embarrassing necessity, perhaps, but far removed from the heart of the Christian life.

The Bible is full of declarations that God, as Creator, is the source of all our blessings and the ultimate owner of all things. Psalm 24 begins:

> The earth is the Lord's and the fullness thereof,
> the world and those who dwell therein;
> for he has founded it upon the seas,
> and established it upon the rivers.

Everything that is good and helpful is a gift from God, given not because we deserve it but because God's love toward us overflows into giving. Even our capacity to work and earn money is built on gifts that we did not do anything to earn: intelligence, talent, health, and the opportunity for education. Real stewardship begins with the grateful acceptance of God's love and blessing. It is a grace born in response to what God has done for us. It is our love for God overflowing in practical ways into every area of life.

The idea that linking money to the spiritual life is somehow wrong finds very little warrant in Scripture. From the earliest days men and women brought things that were precious to them for sacrifice to Yahweh. Times of celebration, thanksgiving, and penitence were marked with gifts. Worship without sacrifice was unthinkable. The Old Testament prophets had no hesitation about taking the people to task about their stewardship. They preached that God's claim of life was total and absolute. It extended beyond the traditional rituals of religion to how one did business and earned and spent money.

Jesus' perceptive comment, "Where your treasure is, there will your heart be also" (Matt. 6:21), sets the tone for New Testament teachings on stewardship. It is interesting to note just how many of Jesus' teachings, sayings, and parables have to do with money and possessions. Again and again he stresses that faith cannot be separated from the affairs of everyday life. His parables are filled with the imagery of economics: a woman searching for a coin, a merchant buying a perfect pearl, a man leaving money with his servants to invest while he goes on a journey. In the vision of the Judgment Day found in Matthew 25, Jesus' identification with the poor is such that it must have direct economic impact on those who love him. Finally, the cross confronts us with the ultimate picture of sacrificial giving and calls us to commit all we are and have to the service of our Savior.

The book of Acts tells how the gospel influenced the first Christians in their use of possessions:

> Now the company of those who believed were of one heart and soul, and no one said that any of the things which he possessed were his own, but they had everything in common. . . . There was not a needy person among them, for as many as were possessors of lands or houses sold them, and brought the proceeds of what was sold and laid it at the apostles' feet; and distribution was made to each as any had need. (Acts 4:32–35)

The apostle Paul spent considerable time and effort during his ministry encouraging the grace of liberality among his congregations. He praised the churches in Macedonia which, though very poor themselves, gave freely to aid the Christians in famine-stricken Jerusalem. These passages echo the message of the whole Bible: God's love demands the best of ourselves and our possessions in response. They make it clear that stewardship is more than simply raising money to keep the church going. Rather it is a lifestyle of grace that

> should take the form, in part, of giving a worthy proportion of [our] income to the church of Jesus Christ, of giving [our]selves in dedication to God, of giving service to others in God's behalf, thus worshiping the Lord with all [we] have and are. Furthermore, all not given more directly to God should be used as a Christian testimony to God and to the world.[1]

Presbyterian Stewardship

To be a Presbyterian is to be in relationship with other Presbyterians all over the world. We are not individual congregations choosing to associate with one another in order to accomplish certain tasks; rather we are the body of Christ, unified and unbroken. The Presbyterian Church is

> a spiritual commonwealth bound together by a series of ascending [councils] which are in subjection to one another in the Lord. . . . Although its members worship in local congregations in different places, these congregations are parts of one whole, elements of one church, organs of one body.[2]

It is because of this relationship that we send money collected in the congregation to presbytery, synod, and General Assembly. We are participating in the unity and mission of the larger church through our gifts. This participation takes a number of different forms, including general mission giving, special offerings, and per capita assessments.

Mission Giving. The Form of Government charges the session to lead "the congregation in participating in the mission of the whole church" [G-3.0201c]. As Presbyterians, our opportunities for mission begin at our own doorstep, but they extend across the entire earth. It is because of these opportunities that sessions budget part of the offerings of the people for mission giving to the wider church.

All councils are responsible for adopting a mission budget to support the work of the church in their area [G-3.0113]. The mission budget of the General Assembly supports the mission of the church at the national and worldwide level. Money for these budgets comes from the gifts of each local congregation. Through giving to mission budgets and special offerings, Presbyterians on the local level have the opportunity to take part in the wider ministry of the church. They support, among other things, children's homes and retirement communities for the elderly. They fund the work of missionaries in dozens of countries. They provide for a denominational church school curriculum and resources for youth ministry. They provide food for the hungry, hospital care for the sick, and resettlement help for refugees. On the presbytery level, mission funds might be used to help operate a homeless shelter or home for battered women. Many presbyteries have camps that are used in their ministry and funded by mission giving. Mission giving may provide for resource people to staff the presbytery and to develop programs of nurture and mission. Participation in all these ministries through giving to mission budgets makes our oneness in Christ a living reality.

Giving to general mission budgets falls into two categories: undesignated giving and designated giving. Undesignated gifts go into the general budgets of the councils to support their mission and program. Designated giving is targeted by the donors to go toward specific objectives—the presbytery's new church development program and the Theological Education Fund, to cite two examples. Both types of giving have their place in the practice of Christian stewardship.

Undesignated gifts make possible the day-to-day operation and ministry of the denomination as a whole. Without strong undesignated giving, much of the PC(USA)'s nationwide and worldwide presence would cease. Designated giving, on the other hand, helps people get involved in and support a particular area of mission. It develops personal interest in mission and enthusiasm for stewardship. The session should promote strong undesignated giving while at the same time offering judiciously chosen opportunities for designated giving.

The *Book of Order* places the responsibility for determining the distribution of the congregation's benevolences on the session [G-3.0205]. This provision refers not only to deciding where such funds shall go but also to determining what proportion of the congregation's offerings is allocated to mission beyond the local church. In allocating the amount to be distributed to causes beyond the congregation, the session should take very seriously the responsibility of the congregation for participation in the mission of the whole church. A tithe of one dollar of benevolence going outside the congregation for every ten dollars of current receipts is a good goal for sessions to begin with.

Special Offerings, Emergency Appeals, and Campaigns. In addition to general mission funds, the councils of the church also approve the taking of special offerings for specific purposes. These offerings are not counted toward fulfillment of one's pledge toward the church budget but are "over-and-above" gifts, focusing on a particular area of need or mission. Collections for support of racial-ethnic schools and those for ministerial relief, along with the One Great Hour of Sharing offering, are examples of special offerings approved by the General Assembly. A synod might authorize a special offering for the purpose of new church development. A presbytery might decide to finance its hunger program in this way. These offerings are usually received on a continuing basis at particular times of year.

Occasionally emergency needs arise, and offerings are taken to meet these needs. These offerings are usually one-time collections for specific purposes, such as responding to a disaster. These offerings can be authorized by any council as necessary, and they also are over-and-above gifts.

From time to time congregations find it necessary to raise large amounts of money for certain purposes such as building new buildings or supporting ministry or mission projects. They may do this through asking the members to give a special offering for this purpose. This kind of appeal for special funds is called a campaign. Institutions of the church such as seminaries and colleges will also have special campaigns to build new buildings or create endowment funds. Before an institution solicits such funds from congregations or sessions, it should seek the approval of the presbytery responsible for that district. Campaigns are not special offerings per se, but they are collections over and above the regular budget, for specific purposes. While supporting the mission thrust of the whole church through general mission funding, Presbyterians are able to become involved with particular aspects of the work through these special offerings, appeals, and campaigns.

Churches receive many requests for money for good causes. It is the responsibility of the session to review these requests and to decide which special offerings will be collected from the congregation. In doing so, the session should give serious consideration to requests from its own presbytery and synod and the General Assembly. After the offerings have been received, the session has the responsibility to see that the funds are distributed for the proper causes and that the congregation is kept informed [G-3.0205].

Per Capita Monies. This term, literally meaning "by heads," refers to a voluntary apportionment used to finance the meetings and ecclesiastical work of councils above the level of the session. The General Assembly in particular depends on per capita monies. Most presbyteries and synods also use this form of funding. Generally, councils set the amount of the per person asking annually, and the money is received by local congregations and then passed on to presbytery, synod, and General Assembly.

Per capita funding generally pays for the expenses of the meetings of these councils, including meals, housing, and travel for commissioners. This allows all persons to participate in the government of the church regardless of their financial status, making for broader participation. Per capita funds also enable the work of many of the administrative committees and commissions of the church. For example, on the General Assembly level these funds cover the expenses of the nominating committee and the permanent judicial commission. The Office of the General Assembly and some of our denomination's ecumenical activities are also financed in this way.

Stewardship Development and the Session

The *Book of Order* places the responsibility for nurturing the grace of stewardship in the congregation squarely on the session. Even in churches where part of this responsibility has been delegated to a board of trustees or to deacons, the session is still responsible to oversee their work. The session is specifically charged with "encouraging the graces of generosity and faithful stewardship of personal and financial resources" [G-3.0201c]. Without generous gifts of time, talents, and money, God's mission through the church cannot go forward. On a personal level, faith grows stale without a constant outpouring of gratitude to God in practical form. Stewardship development is a primary duty of the session as a whole and of teaching and ruling elders as individuals.

There are many ways that the session can fulfill this responsibility, and two deserve particular mention. First, ruling elders should be leaders in personal stewardship. As the 2009-2010 *Book of Order* says: "Those duties which all Christians are bound to perform by the law of love are especially incumbent upon ruling elders because of their calling to office and are to be fulfilled by them as official responsibilities" [G-6.0304]. Ruling and teaching elders should be role models to the congregation in the areas of stewardship and sacrificial giving. If the leadership of the session in this area is weak, if leaders are "preaching" something they do not practice, the whole mission of the church will suffer.

Those approached about being nominated for the ordered ministry of ruling elder should be informed about and give earnest consideration to the stewardship responsibilities of the position before they accept. Ruling elders should be tithers or serious proportionate givers moving toward tithing. Their use of the rest of their possessions should reflect God's ownership of the whole. New ruling elders should look upon their training period as a time to review their giving of money as well as time and talents to the church. They should take seriously the biblical teaching that God will provide for those who respond to the call to do God's will. The giving of a faithful proportion of one's income to God's church is as much a duty of ruling elders as is serving Communion or visiting the sick.

A second important responsibility of the session in the area of stewardship development is sharing information about the mission of the wider church with the congregation. The session is the vital link between the congregation and the rest of the body of Christ. Information flows through the session into the congregation. This information stimulates the giving that makes the mission of the wider church possible.

The church budget should be set up in such a way that the mission of the church is clearly represented to the congregation. Announcements during worship or a regular time for mission education can be used to communicate information about the work of the wider church. Articles in the church newsletter, special programs using films or speakers, and subscriptions to denominational periodicals are all ways in which the session can help people understand what happens to their dollars beyond the local church.

It has been tradition in some areas for the session to delegate much of its financial and stewardship responsibility to the deacons or the board of trustees. Along this line, the *Book of Order* does provide that deacons "shall assume other duties as may be delegated to them by the session" [G-2.0202]. It is clear, however, that the *Book of Order* intends stewardship as related to mission and benevolence to be an important and primary duty of the session. This responsibility is so essential to the spiritual welfare and mission of the church that it deserves constant close attention.

Stewardship and Financial Management[3]

As the job of stewardship development in the congregation begins to bear fruit and the offerings are received, it is up to the session to closely oversee the management of these funds. The session is morally and legally responsible for the correct administration and disbursement of the people's gifts. The session must take its financial duties seriously, using all the means at its disposal to carry out this trust with integrity. Sloppy or unwise management of the congregation's offerings makes the congregation mistrust the session.

The *Book of Order* [G-3.0113] touches on a number of points that relate to the fiscal responsibilities of all councils. These include requiring all councils to prepare and adopt a mission budget, to keep accurate financial records, to carry out a full financial review each year, and to handle all designated gifts correctly. In addition, the session is required to see that offerings are correctly counted and recorded, to elect and oversee the work of a treasurer (unless this oversight is delegated to the deacons), and to make sure that it receives reports on church funds at least annually.

The Church Budget. In the simplest terms, a church budget shows how much money the church expects to receive in a given period of time or for a particular purpose and how it intends to spend that money. In a broader sense, however, a budget is a reflection of values, a statement of goals, an authorization to spend money, and a restraint on spending.

Every budget, whether of a family, a business, or a church, reveals the values of those who drew it up. A family that decides not to budget the cost of a new car this year in favor of putting the money into savings for future college costs is saying something about what is important. A business that budgets gifts to charitable and cultural organizations in the community is making a statement of values. In much the same way, the priorities of a congregation are revealed in its budget.

Try analyzing your congregation's budget in terms of the values it reflects. Compare the amount spent for operating expenses (utilities, supplies, and so on) with the amount spent for ministry and mission. Compare what the church gives for mission beyond the church with what it keeps for ministry inside the congregation. How does your church budget speak to the needs of your community? How does it reflect the priorities and mission of the wider church? What budget item has the largest allotment of funds? Is this item really one that most people would consider a primary priority of the church? Budgets talk, and questions like these can help you hear what your church budget is saying.

Budgets are also statements of a congregation's goals. Goals are concrete and specific things that the church wants to accomplish. Building a new sanctuary, recruiting and training new church school teachers, starting a shepherding program, or helping ten people come to know Christ in the next year are examples of goals. While some of the work of the church can be done by volunteers with little expense involved, most goals require some sort of funding. Even if the goal is simply to keep the doors open and provide weekly services of worship, certain basic expenses must be covered. A budget that reflects the stated goals of the congregation helps to focus attention on those goals and to make sure that the resources are available to accomplish them.

Budgeting should be preceded by an intentional process of evaluation and planning. The questions we ask are crucial. What does God's call for us look like now? What new opportunities for mission have arisen? What new needs have been discovered? Is the church growing or languishing?

What programs have been successful in the past year? What programs have not? Where does the church want to be a year from now? What methods will it use to get there? Specific goals arise out of this kind of questioning. Once they have been discerned through reflection, research, and prayer, goals are then ordered according to priority. Funds are budgeted as necessary to accomplish them. If this kind of budget is shared with the congregation, they will have a clearer idea of where their church, and their money, is going.

The budget is also an authorization to spend money. If the session had to vote on every expenditure of funds, little else would get done around the church. On the other hand, there has to be some control over disbursements if the session is to be a responsible steward. The budget, duly approved by the session, permits specified persons to spend money on behalf of the church to carry out its programs on a day-to-day basis. For instance, if the worship committee has a budget item for music supplies, it can spend that money on printed music, choir robes, music folders, or any other music-related item without going to the session for approval. The original adoption of the budget gave them this authority.

The budget also serves as a restraint on spending. Many people have gotten into financial trouble because they did not keep track of how much they were spending. Churches too can get into difficulty when there are no clear financial limits. A budget provides a kind of fiscal safety net, helping to ensure that the funds provided by the congregation are being used as intended to carry out the church's program.

It is the session's duty to "establish the annual budget" [G-3.0205]. In the Presbyterian Church, the congregation does not vote on the entire budget. The session prepares the budget and presents it to the congregation for information. Although the congregation may make recommendations to the session about various budget items, it votes only on changes in the pastor or pastors' terms of call [G-1.0503]. These include increases or decreases in compensation and the addition or deletion of benefits. The session must present any changes in terms of call to the congregation so that they can exercise this right. Otherwise, all decisions relating to the budget, including the allocation of mission funds, are the responsibility of the session.

Supervision of the Work of the Treasurer. G-3.0205 states that "the session shall elect a treasurer for such term as the session shall decide and shall supervise his or her work or delegate that supervision to a board of deacons or trustee. Those in charge of various congregational funds shall report at least annually to the session and more often as requested." Here again it is clear that the session is the steward of the gifts of the congregation. This section of the *Book of Order* goes on to say that the following standards of financial procedure shall be observed without fail:

the counting and recording of all offerings by at least two
duly appointed persons, or a fidelity bonded person;
the keeping of adequate books and records to reflect all
financial transactions, open to inspection by authorized church officers at reasonable times;
periodic reporting of the financial activities to the board or
boards vested with financial oversight at least annually.

These procedures do not reflect distrust of any person in the church. Rather, they protect those who handle the church's money and provide for orderly lines of accountability and communication.

The status of the current operating fund of the church should be reported to the session regularly. At the very least, these reports should include a statement of actual income for the period, in comparison with the anticipated budgeted income. They should include expenses in major program categories, compared with budgeted funds for those programs. They should also include the status of all ongoing benevolence commitments. A year-end statement of income and expenses should include budgeted figures for the year, actual figures for the year, and actual figures for the preceding year. Such statements can be very simple in form, but their purpose is to let the session gauge the financial health of the church and how far it has progressed toward meeting its goals.

Financial Reviews. A financial review is an examination of financial records for the purpose of verifying that all financial transactions have been properly carried out and recorded. After completion of the required yearly review, the results should be reported promptly to the session. Churches with more complicated financial affairs may contract with professionals for their audit. A church with several members who are knowledgeable about accounting (and not otherwise involved in keeping the church's books) could be appointed to serve as the financial review committee. None of these people should be related to the treasurer(s) [G-3.0113].

The financial review serves to certify the financial statements of the church, verify the propriety of the entries made throughout the year, and make certain that all the items of income received and disbursed during the period have been recorded in the books of account."[4] As with financial reports, these review procedures are not meant to show suspicion of anyone; rather, they protect those who do the church's financial record keeping. Anyone can make a mistake, and a review simply brings any mistakes to light so that they can be corrected. This accepted practice in the world of business can help the church manage its money more correctly and efficiently.

Financial Reports to the Congregation. The *Book of Order* says that the session has the responsibility to provide full information to the congregation relating to its collection and disbursement of authorized offerings [G-3.0205]. While the congregation is not entitled to vote on the entire budget or many other financial decisions, it must still be kept informed as to the status of the church's finances. People want to know about the financial health of the church, and regular reports can instill confidence and stimulate giving. They help inspire the feeling that the session is doing its best to be a good steward of the funds contributed by the congregation. Far too often a congregation is kept in the dark about money matters until a crisis arises and an appeal of some sort has to be made. This gives the impression that the church's finances are being managed poorly. If the session informs the congregation of the church's ongoing financial situation, many of these crisis appeals can be avoided, and those that are necessary because of unusual circumstances will probably receive a better response.

Regular reports should show information about income and expenditures, especially as correlated to the budget. A number of important ratios are also helpful: the per member giving rate (gift income divided by church membership), the ratio of pledged income to giving units, and the ratio of benevolences (money used in mission beyond the membership) to program and operating expenses. These figures could be presented in comparison to those of other Presbyterian churches of similar size, to give the congregation an idea of where they stand in stewardship. Just as this information is extremely helpful to the session as it evaluates and makes plans for the future, so it is helpful to the congregation's understanding of the work of the church.

Handling of Designated Gifts. In a very real sense, money given to the church is given in trust. In a trust agreement there are three parties involved: donor, trustee, and beneficiary. The trustee has the responsibility to make sure that the money is used by the beneficiary as the donor intended. In the situation where a church receives funds, the session is put in the position of being both beneficiary (on behalf of the church) and trustee. As trustee, it is the moral and legal duty of the session to see that the intention of the giver is carried out. In the case of a gift to the current operating budget of the church, the session has the responsibility to ensure that the program represented by the budget is carried out in the way that was indicated to the congregation when the gift was made. In the case of a gift designated or specified for a particular purpose, the session has clear responsibility to ensure that the gift is used as was intended. For instance, in the second example at the beginning of this chapter, the question was raised as to whether the session could use money that had been donated toward the purchase of a new organ to make up a shortfall in current operating income. Deficits of this kind are embarrassing and troublesome, and it is very tempting to use restricted gifts to make up the amount needed. However, this is a clear violation of the intent of the donors, who gave the money with the understanding that it would be used for a specified purpose. The session would be abusing its position as trustee of these funds if it used them to pay the pastor's salary without the express permission of the donor.

Situations of unintentional abuse can be avoided by keeping designated contributions entirely separate from gifts to the current operating budget. A different bank account for these special gifts is strongly recommended. Into this account could be placed all specified memorial gifts, as well as the proceeds from special offerings for various causes. It is also a good practice to place a percentage of the weekly offering equal to the church's pledged benevolence commitments into this special account, for disbursement of benevolences either monthly or quarterly.

Good financial management is good stewardship by the session. Even though the church is a nonprofit corporation, appropriate business practices should be used to manage more effectively the gifts given by the congregation to the glory of God. The discussion above is only the briefest survey of church business management principles. Those assigned specific duties in regard to the church's finances should make a more detailed study of the subject.

The Session and Church Property

Among the responsibilities of the session listed in the Form of Government is "managing the physical property of the church for the furtherance of its mission" [G-3.0201c]. Considering that a good part of a congregation's resources are generally invested in its buildings and property, this duty is an important one. It becomes even more important in light of the fact that this management is carried out not only on behalf of the local congregation but also for the wider church.

Property Held in Trust. G-4.0203 states:

All property held by or for a congregation, a presbytery, a synod, the General Assembly, or the Presbyterian Church (U.S.A.), whether legal title is lodged in a corporation, a trustee or trustees, or an unincorporated association, and whether the property is used in programs of a congregation or of a higher council or retained for the production of income, is held in trust nevertheless for the use and benefit of the Presbyterian Church (U.S.A.).

This means that while the congregation or council holds title to its property, it also accepts certain restrictions on the rights of ownership.

This view of the ownership of church property stems from our relational form of church government and our belief in the unity of the church. As the *Book of Order* says, "The particular congregations of the Presbyterian Church (U.S.A.) wherever they are, taken collectively, constitute one church, called the church" [F-3.0201]. We are not separate churches with a voluntary affiliation with one another; together we are one church, bound together in unity by Jesus Christ. Each congregation of this one church is entrusted to manage its property for the good of the entire Presbyterian Church (U.S.A.).

This basic principle works itself out in a number of ways in relation to the property of congregations. If a congregation leaves the denomination, its property is received by presbytery (unless it has been dismissed to another denomination with its property), which continues to hold it or disposes of it for the benefit of the wider church [G-4.0204]. If a church is dissolved by presbytery or ceases to exist from some other cause, again the presbytery receives the property on behalf of the denomination. In the case of a schism or split in the church, the presbytery has the responsibility to decide which faction (if either)

> is entitled to the property because it is identified by the presbytery as the true church within the Presbyterian Church (U.S.A.). This determination does not depend on which faction received the majority vote within the congregation at the time of the schism. [G-4.0207]

Further, a congregation cannot "sell, mortgage, or otherwise encumber" its land, buildings, or facilities without having presbytery's permission in writing. Permission is necessary when a congregation wishes to buy or otherwise acquire real property that has a mortgage or condition attached. This written permission must be secured by the session before a closing may take place. Also when a church wishes to lease its sanctuary or to lease any of its property for more than five years, written permission from presbytery must be granted [G-4.0206a, b].

The purpose of these provisions is not to hamper the congregation in its exercise of power granted in G-1.0503 in relation to "buying, mortgaging, or selling real property." Neither is their intent to alienate the local church's property from the normal control of the congregation. They simply acknowledge the interest of the wider church in the property held in trust by the congregation. Presbytery is the agent of the Presbyterian Church (U.S.A.), which makes sure that what is being done with such property is not contrary to the interests of the denomination.

Exemptions. While the principle of property held in trust for the wider church holds true, the *Book of Order* allows some exceptions to the specific provisions about obtaining presbytery's permission stated above. These exceptions apply only to a congregation that was not bound by "a similar provision of the constitution of the church of which it was a part" [G-4.0208] (this would generally be a PCUS congregation) before reunion. Such congregations must have requested an exemption relating to selling, encumbering, or leasing church property within eight years after reunion (before June 10, 1991). The congregation must have voted to be excused from the new provision at a regularly called congregational meeting. The congregation must have notified its presbytery of this vote. Such a congregation is excused from specific provisions of G-4.0206a, b and is instead able to buy, sell, mortgage, and lease its property without the approval of presbytery [G-4.0208]. Congregations that have claimed this exemption are still bound by the provisions of G-4.0203, .0204, .0205, .0207 in our current *Book of Order.*

Good Stewardship of the Church's Property. The session's responsibility to serve as a faithful steward of the church's resources extends beyond purely financial matters to the management of the real property of the church. This stewardship is important because money saved in the operation of the church buildings and facilities can be used to increase ministry and mission.

A full discussion of the many areas involved in managing church property is not within the scope of this book. There are, however, certain basics that deserve mention. All councils, including the session, are required to purchase adequate insurance coverage to protect its buildings, programs, staff, and elected and appointed leaders [G-3.0112]. This coverage should be based on accurate professional advice and brought up to date on a regular basis. Any major improvements to the facilities increase their value, and this increase should be reflected in the valuation. Damage to a church by fire or other natural disaster is unfortunate; insurance coverage inadequate to repair the damage or to rebuild can be tragic.

Those directly responsible for managing the church's property under session's supervision should also be good stewards of natural resources. High electric or gas bills drain a church's budget of money that could be used for ministry and mission. Every church should have its buildings evaluated by the local utility company or other appropriate agency and implement as many energy-saving suggestions as possible.

The session is responsible for "managing the physical property of the congregation for the furtherance of its mission" [G-3.0201c]. Part of this responsibility is setting policies for the use of the church buildings both by members and by persons or groups outside the membership of the church. What will be the criteria for deciding if an outside group can use the church? Who will make that decision? What fee will be charged? Will nonreligious groups be permitted to meet there? Can nonmembers use the sanctuary and fellowship hall for weddings? Can alcoholic beverages be served at social occasions in the church buildings or on the grounds? Where is a "no smoking" rule in effect? All these questions should be considered in a comprehensive policy for the use of church facilities.

Along the lines of being good stewards of the church's property, the session could also consider the possibility of letting community service organizations have access to unused space in the church during the week for a nominal fee sufficient to cover utilities and the costs of using the buildings. This is a way to broaden the contacts and ministry of the church in the community as well as to make better use of buildings. Churches have been known to house counseling centers, health clinics, public welfare offices, elder daycare programs, religious broadcasting studios, and Planned Parenthood offices. A building that is full of people all week long, rather than just on Sunday, is a sign that the session is practicing good stewardship of its facilities.

Incorporation and Trustees

The *Book of Order* requires [G-4.0101] that individual churches form and maintain a corporation if the laws of its state allow it to do so. A corporation is a group of people who are legally authorized to act as a single person. The main characteristic of corporations that is of interest to churches is limited liability. This means that individual members of the church or of the session are not held responsible for the corporation's debts or other obligations. Laws governing incorporation and the functions of corporations vary from state to state. Legal advice is often helpful in matters related to incorporation.

Active members of the congregation are members of the church corporation and have the right to vote in corporation business meetings. The corporation has the power to receive, hold, encumber, manage, and transfer property, real or personal, for the congregation, provided that in buying, selling, and mortgaging real property, the trustees shall act only after the approval of the congregation, granted in a duly constituted meeting; to accept and execute deeds of title to such property; to hold and defend title to such property; to manage any permanent special funds for the furtherance of the purposes of the church, all subject to the authority of the session and under the provisions of the Constitution of the Presbyterian Church (U.S.A.).

Trustees are the agents of the corporation who handle its business and carry out its orders. The pastor, not being a member of the corporation, cannot serve as a trustee. However, pastors may be invited to serve as advisers to the trustees. In unincorporated churches, trustees are elected from the active membership by the congregation. Their terms of service shall be governed by the section of the Form of Government that details terms of ruling elders and deacons [G-2.0404]. Trustees always function under the review and control of the session.

Stewardship involves almost every part of the church's life and work. It begins as a personal response of love and gratitude to God and flows outward to enable a worldwide witness in God's name. It is the duty of the session to challenge the congregation with the importance of stewardship, to nurture the grace of liberality in its people, and to serve as a responsible steward of the church's resources. Time and efforts invested in these tasks will bear rich rewards in the ministry and life of the church.

Questions for Reflection and Discussion

1. Jesus spoke often about possessions and God's call on ours. How often is there conversation, teaching, or preaching on this topic in your congregation?

2. How do you feel about this chapter's assertion that church leaders should tithe or be working toward the goal of tithing?

3. What percentage of the undesignated money received by your congregation is spent to carry on mission outside the congregation?

4. How often are your congregation's financial records audited? Does your congregation have insurance for the replacement value of your buildings? When was the last time an energy audit was conducted in your buildings?

Chapter Twelve

MEETINGS OF COUNCILS AND OF THE CONGREGATION

A meeting of the session of Green Pastures Presbyterian Church had been called for the last Sunday in December to approve the budget for the new year. Because of heavy snow, only the pastor and two out of ten session members were able to attend the meeting. "Why don't we call the ones who couldn't get here," said one of the ruling elders, "and if they give the budget their OK, let's go ahead and vote on it tonight. What would be wrong with that?"

Pastor Franklin had just left on a tour of the Holy Land when the clerk of session got a call from the leader of the youth fellowship. "We are planning to have Communion at our retreat next weekend," she said. "Rev. Jones, the presbytery's youth consultant, will be with us to lead the service, but somebody just told me that the session has to approve it. Since Mr. Franklin is out of town, I guess that means that you are in charge. Would you call a session meeting this Sunday after church to approve our Communion service?"

The Importance of Meetings

Many a weary ruling elder, sitting in a session meeting that threatened to drag on into the late evening, has wondered if it would not be better to let the pastor make all the decisions and be done with it. Presbyterian polity, however, has always insisted that church government is best exercised by groups of people who meet together to seek the guidance of the Holy Spirit on matters before them. The *Book of Order* says that church power "is a shared power, to be exercised jointly by presbyters gathered in councils" [F-3.0208]. Therefore, the power to make most decisions in the Presbyterian Church is assigned to councils of elected leaders. The congregation also retains the right to make decisions in certain areas [G-1.0503]. This power is exercised in duly constituted congregational meetings.

The power of councils to make decisions is not an unlimited one, however. Councils are not allowed to do everything they wish. Instead, they are bound by the church's Constitution, particularly by the provisions in the *Book of Order*, as they make decisions. The Constitution seeks to set the limits of power and to ensure that all decisions reached are fair and in accord with Presbyterian beliefs and practice.

An important part of the duty of presbyters is to function as decision makers in meetings of councils. This is done through an orderly process of prayer, discussion, and voting. Through this process the life, mission, and program of the church at all levels are shaped. In order to function effectively as decision makers, the presbyters must know the rules by which meetings of councils operate. This chapter will focus on the constitutional provisions for meetings of session, presbytery, synod, and the General Assembly, as well as those particular rules governing meetings of the congregation. It will also touch briefly on some general considerations relating to effective functioning in meetings.

Consensus and Conflict

In the ideal situation, there would be one perfect answer to every issue, and everyone would recognize it as such. In such a situation, debate and voting would be unnecessary, because all those involved would be in agreement. Many times, particularly where small numbers of people are involved, a group can come to agreement fairly easily. In session meetings, for example, much routine business can be disposed of by common consent. But such is not always the case. As the Historic Principles of Church Order state: "there are truths and forms with respect to which men [sic] of good characters and principles may differ" [F-3.0105]. Differences of opinion are to be expected whenever people gather to make decisions.

The hoped-for goal of decision making is to come to a consensus on an issue, that is, to find an answer to which the whole group can give its consent. To this end the group engages in discussion and debate. Persons who feel strongly about the issue try to persuade others to see things their way. Compromise answers are proposed to try to bridge the gap between differing positions. It often happens that through the process of debate an answer is produced that is better than any of the original suggestions. The group has agreed on an answer, and a vote on the matter (often unanimous) simply affirms its common judgment. Presbyterians believe that this process is one of the ways the Holy Spirit works in the life of the church.

There are times, however, when it is not possible to find an answer on which everyone can agree. After debate and discussion, there are still conflicting opinions. In this situation, the purpose of the vote is to determine the will of the majority, for in our Presbyterian polity "a majority shall govern" [F-3.02 footnote]. The decision of the council binds all its members to act accordingly, regardless of their personal opinion or vote on the matter. If a member thinks that the body has acted in a manner contrary to the church's Constitution, he or she may protest or dissent [G-3.0105]. In cases of extreme disagreement, a case of process may be brought against the council (see the Rules of Discipline).

Discernment. Most of the work of church councils can usually be done by consensus or through a process of prayerful discussion and vote during the meeting. There are, however, significant situations when God's will is not clear to everyone and we must work to understand it. This is when it is helpful to be familiar with the spiritual discipline of discernment. An intentional process of discernment is most appropriate when the matter at hand has long-term consequences, when there are different views on the subject or a variety of choices to be considered, and when the circumstances allow time for working through the matter instead of requiring a quick decision. One of the things that makes church councils different from nonchurch groups is practicing this way of decision making that intentionally seeks to be in the flow of God's will. In practicing discernment as a way of making decisions, councils are acting on our belief that

> God is the creator, redeemer, and sustainer of this world and therefore its rightful ruler;
> God's will for us is good will and we can trust God's faithfulness in good times and in bad;
> God cares what we do and calls us to live in this world in ways that advance God's will being done on earth as it is in heaven;
> The God who calls us into discipleship will give us the resources, guidance, and spiritual power to do God's will;
> The power and grace of God is made manifest in our weakness, so that God can redeem our mistakes and use our failures for God's glory and purposes.
> The prime goal of discernment is not attaining moral perfection but rather partnering with God in the ongoing reconciliation of the world.

It is most helpful to learn about discernment and even practice using it in meetings before a major issue arises. Many good books are available on the subject. In fact, the most helpful practice is to begin using discernment to decide matters in one's own life and family first. Then the moves and postures of discernment can be brought into the council meeting and used to good effect. The practice of discernment as a way of life and also in meetings of councils has the potential to transform both leaders and congregations.

Types of Meetings

The *Book of Order* mentions two types of meetings of councils: stated and special [G-3.0203]. *Stated meetings* are those that are scheduled in advance and generally held on a regular basis (the second Tuesday of the month, for example). At these meetings the council can act on any business, including new business that arises. The bylaws of the council usually specify how many stated meetings the body shall have in a year and may specify when they shall be held. The Constitution specifies a minimum number of stated meetings per year for each council. Notice for these meetings generally goes out through the council's normal channels of communication.

Special meetings are held to deal with business that cannot wait until the next stated meeting or with matters requiring more time than a stated meeting provides. A session, for instance, may call a special meeting to receive new members into the church if the next stated meeting of the session is too far in the future. A presbytery might have a special meeting to examine candidates for ordination, in order to give this important business extra attention. Special meetings of synods and the General Assembly are seldom held, but they can be called if needed.

Whenever a special meeting of a congregation or council is called, the intended business must be stated clearly in the notice. No new business, or business other than that stated in the call, can be transacted [G-3.0203]. There should be no surprise items on the agenda of special meetings.

Moderators and Clerks

The stated officers that all councils from session to the General Assembly must have are moderator and clerk [G-3.0104]. These offices are functional, not honorary, and their rather modest titles reflect the clear teaching of our polity that Christ alone is head of the church. Officers of councils (other than moderator of the session) are usually elected for limited periods of time, again reflecting our reluctance to invest inappropriate authority in any individual.

Above the session, officers of councils are elected by the councils themselves. The moderator is the presiding officer of the council. It is his or her responsibility to see that meetings are orderly and that the business of the body is conducted with efficiency and fairness. Moderators should be quite familiar with the Constitution of the church, especially the Form of Government, and also with *Robert's Rules of Order Newly Revised*, which is to be used as the parliamentary authority of all councils [G-3.0105].

The moderator convenes and adjourns stated meetings as directed by the group [G-3.0104]. Moderators carry out any duties assigned to them by the council, including those of appointing members to standing committees and making appointments to certain offices or functions. All moderators have the authority needed to run an orderly, efficient, and Christlike meeting. This would include adjourning the meeting summarily if proceedings become disorderly or disrespectful.

Clerks (called stated clerks in councils higher than the session) record and preserve the minutes of meetings and keep rolls of membership and attendance. They present all minutes to the council for approval and submit all records and reports requested by more-inclusive councils. The clerk works closely with the moderator to make meetings run smoothly. Most official communications to a council come to it through its clerk. Clerks are responsible for conveying these communications to their councils and for recording their disposition. The body they are serving determines the term of service of the clerk.

The moderator of the session is always the pastor of the congregation unless there is no installed pastor. The session cannot convene in the absence of the pastor except in cases of sickness or other unusual circumstance. In these cases the Book of Order makes provision for another minister or ruling elder to preside temporarily [G-3.0104].

The pastor-moderator, as presbyter and member of the session, is entitled to vote on all questions that come before the body [G-3.0201]. Other installed teaching elders who are members of session are also entitled to vote. It is our opinion that it is wise for the moderator to make it a practice to vote regularly. In so doing the moderator not only exercises his or her right as a member of the session but also defuses potential charges of favoritism when controversial issues arise and close votes occur.

Ruling elders, whether actively serving on the session of their particular church or not, are eligible to serve as commissioners to and officers of more-inclusive councils. Ruling elders elected moderator of presbytery "shall be enrolled as members during the period of their service," whether or not commissioned by his or her session [G-3.0301]. Further, presbyteries may decide to make other ruling elders serving the presbytery as moderators of commissions or committees members of presbytery during their time of service [G-3.0301].

The clerk of session may also be an inactive ruling elder elected by the session to serve in this capacity for a period of time decided by the session. In this situation the clerk cannot vote because he or she is not a member of the session. However, it would be wise to grant such a clerk the privilege of the floor so that he or she can ask questions in order to ensure that the record of the meeting is complete and accurate.

While the moderator and the clerk are the two stated officers required by the Book of Order, councils may also elect other officers as necessary. These might include assistant or associate stated clerks and vice-moderators.

Parliamentary Procedure

The underlying ideas of general parliamentary proce

1. Everyone is treated with courtesy.
2. One item is dealt with at a time.
3. The majority rules.
4. The majority respects the rights of the minority.
5. Justice for all.
6. No partiality.[1]

These principles are very much in accord with Presbyterian polity and Christian principles. The purpose of parliamentary procedure is to move the business of the body along as swiftly and efficiently as possible while ensuring that everyone is treated fairly. The Form of Government specifies that meetings of councils "shall be conducted in accordance with the most recent edition of *Robert's Rules of Order Newly Revised*, except when this is in contradiction to this Consitution [G-3.0105].

A group may also adopt special rules that apply particularly to that body. Bylaws and standing rules fall into this category. These special rules take precedence over the general rules (such as *Robert's Rules*) when they come into conflict. For example, our church's Constitution specifies that a two-thirds vote is required on certain items of business, while the general parliamentary rules require only a majority. The denomination's constitutional provisions would govern in this case. Therefore any provision of the Presbyterian Church (U.S.A.)'s Constitution overrules any provision in any council's bylaws or standing rules or any provision in *Robert's Rules* with which it may be in conflict.

It is hard to overestimate the helpfulness of a knowledge of parliamentary procedure to those participating in the meetings of councils. For moderators of meetings, it is essential. Ignorance of the rules of order results in much confusion and wasted time and endangers the rights of individuals and the welfare of the group. While a survey of parliamentary procedure is beyond the scope of this book, we urge all presbyters to obtain a copy of the latest *Robert's Rules* along with whatever general and special rules have been adopted by their councils and make a careful study of them. Further, it is helpful for each council to have a parliamentarian whose job it is to know these rules in detail and to offer suggestions about procedure to the group when asked.

The rest of this chapter will survey briefly the provisions in the *Book of Order* relating to meetings of each of the councils and of the congregation. A chart containing this information in condensed form will be found at the end of this chapter.

Congregational Meetings

Participants. When the congregation gathers for a business meeting, all members on the active roll who are present are eligible to speak and to vote. No proxy or absentee voting is allowed in congregational meetings or in any meeting of a council, except in meetings of church corporations where required by civil law. The pastor, as moderator, may speak as necessary to provide information or clarification but, not being a member of the congregation, shall refrain from engaging in debate and shall not vote.

The *Book of Order* does not specify what course a council should take if the matter on the floor results in a tie; therefore the provisions of *Robert's Rules* prevail. Note that since the moderator of a congregational meeting is generally not a member of the congregation, he or she cannot vote to break a tie vote. Visitors at a congregational meeting are not entitled to speak unless the congregation votes to grant them this privilege. The Form of Government does not specify that official visitors from presbytery are to be given the privilege of the floor at congregational meetings, but everything in our relational, representative system of polity points in that direction.

Officers. The officers serving at a congregational meeting are the moderator and secretary. Just as the pastor is the moderator of the session, so is she or he the moderator of the meetings of the congregation. When a church is without a pastor, the person serving as moderator of the session by appointment of presbytery shall moderate congregational meetings. In cases where circumstances are such that the pastor cannot or should not preside, he or she shall invite another teaching elder of the presbytery or someone else authorized by the presbytery to preside.

Congregational meetings also require a secretary whose job it is to record the minutes of the meeting and to see that they are entered in the session's minute book. Ordinarily, the clerk of the session shall serve as the secretary of the congregational meeting. If the clerk is absent or otherwise prevented from serving, one of the very first items on the agenda must be for the congregation to elect someone to serve as secretary and record minutes of the meeting.

Frequency of Meetings. The *Book of Order* requires that congregations meet at least once a year [G-1.0501]. If the church is incorporated, state law may also require that certain meetings be held to conduct the business of the corporation. These may be held in conjunction with the regular annual meeting of the congregation, if state law allows [G-1.0503].

Many churches have made good use of the required annual meeting to draw together and celebrate the life of the congregation over the past year. This is an excellent opportunity for groups in the church to make reports on program and mission. It can be an opportunity to evaluate strengths and weaknesses. It is a chance for members of the congregation to express their thoughts and feelings about how things are going in the church and to share ideas about directions for the future. The meeting should be held at a time that will encourage a large attendance. At the very least, the annual meeting of the congregation should be a time to count the blessings that God has poured out on the people and to give thanks.

When any special congregational meeting is called, the congregation must be informed of the topic of the meeting and given adequate public notice. The Form of Government leaves it up to the congregation to decide what constitutes adequate notice in its situation. It simply specifies that congregations "shall provide by their own rule for minimum notification requirements and give notice at regular services of worship prior to the meeting" [G-1.0502]. This kind of information should be included in the congregation's bylaws.

Quorum. This term refers to the minimum number of eligible voters required to be present in order for business to be transacted. Actions taken in the absence of a quorum are subject to challenge, as specified in *Robert's Rules of Order*. It is the duty of the secretary of the congregational meeting to make sure that a quorum is present and to report this fact to the moderator at the beginning of the meeting. Each congregation sets the number of members that constitute a quorum, and this information should be recorded and made public in bylaws or some other such document.

Business at Congregational Meetings. A congregation is not a council. Therefore it can transact only those items of business specifically given to it by the Constitution. The *Book of Order* [G-1.0503] lists five kinds of business that can be transacted by congregations:

1. matters related to the nominating and electing of ruling elders, deacons, and trustees;
2. matters related to the calling of a pastor, co-pastor, or associate pastor;
3. matters related to changing the pastoral relationship, such as changing a current pastor's terms of call, or requesting or consenting or declining to consent to dissolution of the relationship;
4. matters relating to buying, mortgaging, or selling real property;
5. matters related to other permissive powers of a congregation, such as the decision to use or not use the ordered ministry of deacon, or the request to presbytery for exemption from one or more requirements because of limited size (G-2.0404).

While, on the one hand, the Constitution limits the congregation's decision making to the matters listed above, at the same time it protects the congregation's right to decide these matters free from interference by any council. A session, for instance, cannot buy any property on behalf of the church without the consent of the congregation voting as a corporation, if the church is incorporated. The presbytery cannot insist that a certain person be installed as pastor against the wishes of a congregation. Only under the most extreme conditions and only as specified by the Constitution may a council interfere with the right of a congregation to decide the matters listed above.

Meetings of the Session

Participants. All ruling elders in active service are members of the session during their term of service. The pastor, co-pastors, and associate pastors of the congregation are also members of the session. They are all entitled to speak in meetings and to vote. Other members of the congregation and staff members may be invited to attend session meetings, and if the session votes to allow them to speak, they may do so. They may not vote. The session has the right under *Robert's Rules* to exclude nonmembers from the meeting place and to meet in executive session whenever circumstances indicate the wisdom of doing so. Such circumstances might include discussion of personnel or disciplinary matters.

Meeting Frequency. Stated meetings of the session must be held at least quarterly [G-3.0203]. Special session meetings can be called by the moderator at his or her discretion and must be called if requested in writing by any two session members. The presbytery can also direct the session to convene a meeting for some special business. The *Book of Order* does not specify exactly how much notice is required before a special session meeting can be held. Therefore the session shall decide and record the rule it has made regarding what constitutes adequate notice. The business to be transacted at these meetings must not include any matter not specified in the original call.

Quorum. Sessions can set the rule for their own quorums. Again, this is something that should be included in a church's bylaws. The quorum set shall be stated in terms of a specific number or percentage of ruling elder members of session along with the moderator [G-3.0203].

Meetings of Presbytery

Participants. All ruling elders elected as commissioner by their sessions are voting members of presbytery with the right to speak on the floor and hold office. The Form of Government specifies that teaching elders who are members of presbytery in the active-member or member-at-large categories are entitled to speak, vote, and hold office in presbytery. Honorably retired teaching elders by virtue of being members of presbytery are also entitled to speak, vote and, hold office even though this privilege is not specifically mentioned in G-2.0503c. Others serving presbytery in certain ways may also be given these privileges [G-3.0301]. A presbytery may vote to allow someone other than a commissioner or corresponding member to speak, but unless this is done, visitors must be silent. No one may vote except presbyter members of that presbytery.

The *Book of Order* states that the balance between ruling and teaching elders should be as nearly even as possible. In order for this to be so, the presbytery shall adopt a way to foster this parity and communicate it to the sessions. In doing this, presbyteries should pay particular attention to *Book of Order* provisions relating to inclusiveness [F-1.0403]. The number of elder commissioners a church is ordinarily entitled to send to presbytery meetings is set by the presbytery.

Meetings and Quorum. The presbytery is required to have at least two stated meetings a year and must also meet when requested by synod. Special meetings of the presbytery may be called in whatever way the presbytery decides is best and sets as its rule [G-3.0304]. The quorum set by the presbytery shall not be less than three teaching elder members of presbytery and three ruling elder commissioners who are members of three different churches.

Meetings of Synod

Participants. Those entitled to vote in synod meetings are commissioners elected by the presbyteries. The commissioners from each presbytery in the synod shall be divided equally between ruling and teaching elders. There must be at least one of each from each constituent presbytery. The plan for electing these commissioners and the ratio of representation between presbyteries is proposed by the synod and must receive the consent of a majority of its constituent presbyteries. G-3.0401 instructs that in making this plan they must be guided by our denomination's principles of inclusiveness and diversity (see also F-1.0403 and G-3.0103). Synod may decide to give those who are members in good standing in other councils of our church or in other Christian churches the privilege of speaking on the floor of synod, but these persons may not vote.

Meetings and Quorum. Synods must hold at least one stated meeting every other year. Special meetings of the synod must be called when so directed by the General Assembly. The synod may also adopt its own rules about when and how to call special meetings [G-3.0405]. As with all meetings of councils, adequate notice as defined by the synod's own rules must be given. The synod decides for itself what its quorum shall be, and this becomes its rule. The minimum required by the Form of Government is ruling and teaching elders in equal numbers representing one-third of its constituent presbyteries or three presbyteries, whichever is larger [G-3.0405].

Meetings of the General Assembly

Participants. Commissioners to the General Assembly are elected by the presbyteries and must include ruling and teaching elders in equal number. Presbyteries are charged to make sure that the commissioners sent to the General Assembly reflect the diversities found in their membership. Each presbytery is eligible to send one teaching elder and one ruling elder to the General Assembly for roughly each 8,000 members, up to 48,000 members. For example, a presbytery with 35,000 members would send ten commissioners, five ruling elder-teaching elder pairs (see G-3.0501 for specifics). Persons other than commissioners seated by the General Assembly may be given the privilege of the floor, but they may not vote in plenary sessions. Much of the work of the General Assembly meeting is guided by the *Standing Rules of the General Assembly*. These rules can be accessed in the publications section of the Office of the General Assembly Web site.

Meeting Frequency and Quorum. As with the synod, the General Assembly must have at least one stated meeting every other year. Special meetings of the General Assembly are extremely rare, and the procedure for such a call is set out in G-3.0503. Sixty days' notice must be given before such meetings. As with other councils, the business for the special meeting must be specifically stated in the call notice. No other business may be considered at the special meeting. Quorum for a General Assembly meeting is one hundred commissioners, half ruling elders and half teaching elders. These commissioners must represent presbyteries in at least one fourth of the church's synods.

Decision making is an important part of the responsibility of the ruling and teaching elders. Much of this decision making takes place in meetings. Presbyterians believe that the Holy Spirit works in and through meetings to shape the life and mission of the church. To be effective participants in these meetings, ruling elders and ministers need a prayerful willingness to know and do God's will as well as knowledge of parliamentary procedure and the PC(USA) Constitution.

Questions for Reflection and Discussion

1. What proportion of the business at an average meeting of your session is decided by consensus? By debate and voting? Is this about the right proportion?

2. Think about a meeting you attended at church or elsewhere where you felt the presence of God. What was it about the meeting that helped you feel that way?

3. In your opinion, what makes for a good meeting?

4. Think about the last time there was a controversial matter before a meeting of your congregation. How was the matter handled? What was the tenor of the debate? Were people given a chance to express a wide range of opinions? How was the matter resolved?

TABLE OF RULES FOR MEETINGS OF COUNCILS AND THE CONGREGATION

	CONGREGATION	SESSION	PRESBYTERY	SYNOD	THE GENERAL ASSEMBLY
WHO MAY CALL MEETINGS	(a) session (b) presbytery (c) session must call when requested by ¹/₄ members on active roll	(a) pastor (b) presbytery (c) pastor must call on request of 2 session members	(a) synod (b) presbytery may call special meetings in accordance with its own rules	(a) General Assembly (b) synod in accordance with its own rules	Moderator (or in the event of incapacipy of Moderator, Stated Clerk) of General Assembly, at the request or with the concurrence of at least ¹/₄ of the teaching elder commissioners of last preceding stated meeting of General Assembly, representing at least 15 presbyteries under jurisdiction of at least 5 synods
REQUIRED NOTICE OF SPECIAL MEETINGS	adequate public notice	"reasonable" when other than routine business is on agenda	in accordance with its own rules	in accordance with its own rules	not less than 60 days
QUORUM	congregations shall provide by rule the quorum necessary to conduct business	sessions shall provide by rule for a quorum for meetings; quorum shall include moderator and either a specific number of ruling elders or specific percentage of those ruling elders in current service on session	3 teaching elders plus 3 ruling elders representing at least 3 congregations, or higher if set by presbytery	synod may set its own quorum, but shall include equal number of ruling elders and teaching elders representing at least 3 presbyteries or ¹/₃ of its presbyteries, whichever is larger	100 commissioners (¹/₂ ministers, ¹/₂ elders) representing at least ¹/₄ of its synods

	CONGREGATION	SESSION	PRESBYTERY	SYNOD	THE GENERAL ASSEMBLY
REQUIRED STATED MEETINGS	once a year	at least quarterly	twice a year	biennially	biennially
WHO IS ELIGIBLE TO VOTE	all active members of the congregation present at either annual or special meetings are entitled to vote	all members of the session (those persons elected by congregation to active service as ruling elders, plus all installed pastors & associate pastors)	teaching elders who are engaged in ministry validated by that presbytery; a member-at-large (as determined by presbytery, G-2.0503a) or honorably retired (G-2.0502); ruling elders commissioned to serve at presbytery (by plan adopted by presbytery and communicated to the sessions regarding how many ruling elders each session should elect as commissioners, G-3.0301); Certified Christian Educators who are ruling elders, engaged in educational ministry under jurisdiction of presbytery (G-2.1103b)	commissioners elected by the presbyteries, at least 1 ruling elder & 1 teaching elder	equal numbers of ruling elders and teaching elders elected by the presbyteries and reflective of diversity w/ in their bounds (F-1.0403, G-3.0103) in the proportions outlined in G-3.0501
OFFICERS	moderator secretary (usually clerk of session)	moderator clerk	moderator stated clerk	moderator stated clerk	moderator stated clerk
BUSINESS	all matters related to G-1.0503	all matters related to G-3.02	all matters related to G-3.03	all matters related to G-3.04	all matters related to G-3.05

Chapter Thirteen

PRESERVING
PEACE
AND PURITY

John Harper is a commissioner to the meeting of Sealand Presbytery. During the meeting, candidates for ordination to the
ordered ministry of teaching elder are examined. As the examinations proceed, it becomes clear that one of the candidates does not
believe in the baptism of infants and does not intend to teach this
doctrine or to administer the sacrament to children. John is very
disturbed when the presbytery votes to ordain the candidate any-
way. What can he do to correct what he feels is an error committed
by his presbytery?

Clearview Presbyterian Church is in turmoil. A small group in
the church, led by a well-respected ruling elder, has decided that
the pastor is not a "born-again Christian" and that she should
be fired. At the request of the pastor, a meeting of the session is
called to discuss the issue. The session gives the pastor a vote of
confidence. However, the ruling elder is not satisfied. In various
ways he continues to disrupt session meetings, to verbally abuse
the pastor and undermine her work, and to spread gossip about
her in the community. What can the session do to help restore
order in the church?

Conflict in the Church

From the earliest days of the church, believers have clashed over issues
of faith and how to live out that faith in the world. The infant church was
often rife with controversy, as a reading of the book of Acts will show. Conflict in the church often arose over things that seem quite trivial to us today,
such as the issue of whether Christians should eat meat that had been
offered first to idols (1 Cor. 8; 10:23–33). In the early decades of the church's
life there were squabbles over whether Gentiles should be allowed to con-
vert to Christianity without being circumcised first, whether Christians
should marry, and whether Christians were bound to keep the Jewish law,
among other questions. Even personalities got involved, causing dissen-
sion in the church at Corinth as "disciples" of various evangelists split the
church into factions.

These conflicts must have been quite painful to those early Christians. It may have seemed to them that the church was coming apart at the seams. Yet, in many cases, something positive emerged from these dark experiences to the benefit of the church. Some of the key doctrines of our faith were forged in the fire of these early controversies. In fact, almost every important facet of Christian belief, from the nature of Christ to the hope of life after death, was a matter for conflict in the ancient church at one point or another.

The book of Acts could almost be read as a manual for conflict resolution in the church. Time and time again differences of opinion and practice arose in the fledgling community. Yet the church was not destroyed by conflict; to the contrary, it often grew stronger because of it. A good example of this is the problem described in Acts 6:1–6. It was the practice of the Christians to provide food for the widows among them who were destitute. The Greek-speaking church members complained that the Greek-speaking widows were being neglected in the distribution of food while the Hebrew-speaking widows were well fed. This conflict put pressure on the apostles, who already had all the work they could handle preaching the gospel and making disciples of new converts. The outcome of this discord was a ministry similar to what we today call the ordered ministry of deacon, and in an epilogue to the story, the Scripture notes that "the word of God increased; and the number of the disciples multiplied greatly in Jerusalem" (Acts 6:7).

Considering human nature and the fact that human beings make up the church, we should not be surprised when conflict arises. People with perfectly good motives and intentions may have conflicting goals. Sincere Christians may confess the same doctrines yet have radically different ideas about how those doctrines should be interpreted and lived out. In these situations, our goal as Christians is reconciliation—restoring harmony and fellowship among those who differ. We believe that today, as in the early church, the Holy Spirit can work through the process of conflict to bring about the will of God. Painful though it may be, conflict can help the church grow and become more creative in its life and ministry.

One of the finest things about our Presbyterian system of government is that it provides fair and efficient means to deal with conflict in the church. Our polity is realistic about life in community: It takes for granted that differences will exist and helps us to deal with those differences in ways that are constructive rather than destructive. Before getting into the particulars of how the system works, it will be helpful to understand some of the underlying principles on which it is based.

Ground Rules for Dealing with Conflict

Our Form of Government makes several important assumptions about how churches and their councils should go about their business. Ruling elders and other leaders are expected to give assent to these basic principles.

Freedom of Conscience. The Declaration of Independence names liberty as one of the inalienable rights of human beings. This, of course, refers to our political freedom. The Bible tells us about another kind of freedom, which belongs to Christians through the death and resurrection of Christ. Christian freedom is freedom from many things, but it is also freedom for a new kind of life. Part of our Christian birthright is a freedom of the mind, a liberty to think freely, to question, even to doubt. This kind of liberty grows out of a loving and obedient relationship to God. Reformed theology has called this intellectual freedom "freedom of conscience," and it is one of the important principles of our system of government. "Freedom of conscience" means that we are freed from demands for slavish, unquestioning obedience. God does not want us to be robots who act according to programmed instructions. God wants us to respond freely in love, to give God our trust, and to follow God's way in willing faith and gratitude. If God does not demand mindless submission from us, neither should the church demand it. The Westminster Confession (XXII, 2) puts it like this:

> God alone is Lord of the conscience, and hath left it free from the doctrines and commandments of men [sic] which are in anything contrary to his Word, or beside it in matters of faith or worship. So that to believe such doctrines, or to obey such commandments out of conscience, is to betray true liberty of conscience; and the requiring an implicit faith, and an absolute and blind obedience, is to destroy liberty of conscience, and reason also.

We are bound by the Word of God and by the authority of the church as it flows from the Word. However, within these bounds we have the right to interpret the Scriptures for ourselves. The door is always open for honest doubt and questioning; we are called to respect the right of others to see things their own way. The Presbyterian system of government always allows room for a "loyal opposition."

Power of Councils and the Constitution. Freedom of conscience, like any other freedom, has its limits. In tension with the Christian's freedom is the power of the church to govern itself and its members. One of the questions asked of leaders at their ordination is, "Will you be governed by our church's polity, and will you abide by its discipline?" [W-4.4003e]. Another question asks if the leader is willing to adopt the confessions of the church as "reliable expositions of what Scripture leads us to believe and do"[W-4.4003c]. To say yes to these questions is to make a commitment to be Presbyterian in the way we express our faith and do our business.

The *Book of Order* [G-2.0105] states:

So far as may be possible without serious departure from [the essentials of the Reformed faith expressed in our church's Constitution], without infringing on the rights and views of others, and without obstructing the constitutional governance of the church, freedom of conscience with respect to the interpretation of Scripture is to be maintained.

This means that we can study the Bible for ourselves and come to our own conclusions about what it means. We are free to have our own opinions on matters of faith and practice. We are free to speak our minds on the floor of church meetings and to seek to persuade other people to see things our way. We can vote as our consciences tell us on any matter. However, when the vote has been taken and the matter decided by a majority, we are bound to follow the decision of the council. We are still entitled to hold opinions that do not agree with the decision, but our actions, including teaching, must be in line with the Constitution of the church and the decision of the council. This tension between the freedom of the individual and the authority of the church maintains the possibility of creative conflict, while assuring that order will be preserved and that the work of the church will go forward. Ours is a system of church government that lets people read the Scripture and interpret it for themselves in freedom before God, but it is also a system that binds us together in a community marked by humility and loving submission.

Mutual Forbearance. The key to making the system work is recognizing that we may not always be right. One of the historic principles of church order as stated in our Form of Government is "that there are truths and forms with respect to which men [sic] of good characters and principles may differ" [F-3.0105]. Christians can agree to disagree at times without sacrificing their integrity or that of the faith. It is this willingness to bow to the decision of the majority that lets conflict be resolved and the work of the church go on.

Our form of church government is based on the idea that God's Spirit moves in and through the actions of the church's councils . Debate, discussion, and orderly decision making are some of the ways we explore the will of God and hear God's voice. We take seriously the idea that "where two or three are gathered in my name, there am I in the midst of them" (Matt. 18:20), and we apply it to meetings of church committees, sessions, presbyteries, and other councils. When we participate in these meetings, we translate our beliefs into action through discussion and the vote. This theology requires that we respect the decision of the group, even though we may disagree with it. We bow to the will of the majority, believing that even if the decision is wrong, God can still bring something good out of our failure.

In times of conflict, it is well to remember that no one has a monopoly on the Spirit of God. The business of the church should always be carried out in a spirit of humility. An open mind and a willingness to be shown where we are in error will do much toward smoothing a troubled situation. The Foundations of Presbyterian Polity states that "it is the duty of private Christians and societies to exercise mutual forbearance toward each other" [F-3.0105]. This means that we should be patient with those who disagree with us and slow to express resentment or to retaliate. This kind of tolerance and respect oils the wheels of our Presbyterian system of government and helps it to work well, even when conflict arises.

Options for Disagreement—Dissent and Protest

There are times when, for conscience' sake, it is necessary to speak out against the decision or action of a council. The Form of Government offers several ways to express disagreement with the majority without beginning judicial process.

A *dissent* is a means of having it recorded in the minutes of a meeting that one voted against a certain decision. Dissenters are listed by name in the official record of the proceedings. The request to dissent must be made during the same session as the objectionable action. A person who wants to dissent should address the moderator of the meeting and say something like: "I dissent from this decision and request that my negative vote be recorded." Only those who voted against a motion, except the moderator if unable to vote [G-3.0105-.0105a] can dissent.

A *protest* is a means for expressing more serious disagreement. While a request for a dissent is simply spoken before the group, a protest is presented to the clerk of the meeting in written form. It should state the date and place of the meeting, the council that took the action being protested, and the reasons for disagreement. The names of those protesting are signed at the bottom. A protest, like a dissent, can be made only by those who voted against an action, except the moderator if unable to vote, and it must be filed before the session of the council is adjourned [G-3.0105b].

The language of a protest should reflect forbearance and respect for the council. If a protest is orderly and respectful, it shall be included in the minutes of the meeting. The value of entering a protest, other than simply for conscience's sake, is that it will draw the objectionable action to the attention of those in more-inclusive councils who are reviewing the minutes of the lower body. The more-inclusive council has the power to investigate the situation and to correct any errors of the lower body. This power of more-inclusive councils is called "administrative review." After a protest has been entered in the minutes, the council has the right to prepare an answer to it and to enter the answer in the minutes. This is the end of the protest. Making a protest in no way gives one permission to act counter to the action of the council. These two options for expressing disagreement with a decision of a council are not means to have the decision changed; they simply register one's disapproval in the minutes of the meeting.

What Is "Discipline"?

One of the sections of our *Book of Order* is called Rules of Discipline. Yet few church members, or even leaders, are clear about what discipline is and how it works in the church. The word "discipline" comes from the Latin word *discere,* to learn. A disciple is one who learns and lives by the teachings of another. To be a disciple of Jesus, a member of the body of Christ, is to agree to live by the example and the teachings of Jesus. Not only our individual lives but also the internal life of the church should reflect Christlike qualities. "Church discipline," simply put, is the church's power to help us live as disciples of Christ.

Discipline has many facets. When we make mistakes or fall into sin, the church has the power to point out what we have done wrong and to call us to repent and to change our ways. When we have neglected our duties as Christians, the church has the power to correct us. When conflict arises, discipline is one of the ways the church restores peace. When scandal threatens, discipline helps to preserve the good name of Christ in the world. Discipline protects the rights of the minority and makes sure that people are treated fairly in the church. Discipline provides for orderly resolution of differences in ways that are "just, speedy, and economical" [D-1.0101]. Discipline is the church's use of power given to it by Christ to guide, control, and nurture its members, as well as to offer constructive criticism to those who do wrong [D-1.0101].

Several centuries ago, especially in Scotland, it was not uncommon for sessions to take church members to task about their conduct. To miss worship regularly was to risk being called before the session and censured in public. This kind of encounter is rare today, but the idea of discipline still leaves a bad taste in the mouths of some. Our polity stresses that discipline is more a positive, loving concern for people than a vengeful system for punishing wrongdoers. Our rules for discipline focus on bringing people to reconciliation with God and one another. Their purpose is to build up the body of Christ. They do this by making sure that people are treated fairly, that conflicts are resolved in an equitable way, and that everyone has a chance to speak and to be heard. Discipline is also a witness to the fact that it means something to be a Christian. It reminds us of our commitments and calls us to live up to them. When our conduct does not measure up to the standards required of disciples, it is the church's duty to correct us in a spirit of love and mercy.

On July 6, 1996, a newly revised Rules of Discipline went into effect. The purpose of the revision was primarily to simplify and clarify procedures and make the rules easier to use. This revision also gave a definition for sexual misconduct to be used in disciplinary cases and provided for the use of mediation in remedial cases.

It is important to note that the first and foundational chapter of the Rules of Discipline points to the biblical obligation to "conciliate, mediate, and adjust differences without strife" [D-1.0103]. Every possible avenue of conflict resolution should be pursued before resorting to judicial process. "It remains the duty of every church member to try (prayerfully and seriously) to bring about an adjustment or settlement of the quarrel, complaint, delinquency, or irregularity asserted, and to avoid formal proceedings under the Rules of Discipline" [D-1.0103].

Judicial Process

From time to time there arises in the church a disagreement so severe or an error so harmful that a dissent or protest is not enough to deal with it. In this case our Rules of Discipline offer the option of solving the problem through judicial process. The Rules of Discipline [D-2.0101] defines judicial process as

the exercise of authority by the councils of the church for:

a. the prevention and correction of irregularities and delinquencies by councils, the Presbyterian Mission Agency,[1] or an entity of the General Assembly (Remedial Cases, D-6.0000);
b. the prevention and correction of offenses by persons (Disciplinary Cases, D-10.0000).

An irregularity is an action or decision of a council that is in error [D-2.0202a]. A delinquency is the neglect of duty or the refusal to carry out responsibilities by a council [D-2.0202b]. Judicial cases that attempt to correct irregularities or delinquencies on the part of councils or the Presbyterian Mission Agency or an agency of the General Assembly are called *remedial cases* [D-2.0202].

An offense is an action or failure to act on the part of an individual—member, ruling elder, deacon, or teaching elder—that is in opposition to the Scriptures or to the Constitution of the church. Cases that aim at correcting or censuring the offenses of individuals are called *disciplinary cases* [D-2.0203].

For example, in the situations at the beginning of the chapter, John Harper could have complained against the action of his presbytery in accepting the candidate for ministry, in an attempt to correct the irregularity. This would involve a remedial case. The session of Clearview Presbyterian Church, in the second situation, could have brought charges against the troublesome ruling elder in an attempt to make him stop damaging the peace of the church. This would involve a disciplinary case.

Judicial process in the church is a very serious matter. As stated in D-1.0101, its purpose is

> to honor God by making clear the significance of membership in the body of Christ; to preserve the purity of the church by nourishing the individual within the life of the believing community; to correct or restrain wrongdoing in order to bring members to repentance and restoration; to uphold the dignity of those who have been harmed by disciplinary offenses; to restore the unity of the church by removing the causes of discord and division; and to secure the just, speedy, and economical determination of proceedings.

Judicial process should not be undertaken lightly or be used to further personal causes. Its sole purpose is to build up the body of Christ by ensuring that people are treated fairly, that correct doctrine and practice are preserved, and that scandal is not allowed to damage the church's reputation. As with all discipline, its function is to correct in a spirit of love and concern, not to punish. Those considering beginning a judicial case are required to exhaust every other option for reconciliation and correction before taking this step.

Above the level of the session, judicial cases are heard and decided by permanent judicial commissions. The Rules of Discipline directs each presbytery, synod, and the General Assembly to elect a permanent judicial commission from among its teaching and ruling elders, membership being divided evenly between the two, as much as possible. The presbytery commission has no fewer than seven members, with no more than one ruling elder member from the same church. Synod's commission has no fewer than eleven members, usually no more than one from the same presbytery. The General Assembly's commission is made up of one member from each of the synods. Members of permanent judicial commissions serve a term of six years, and their expenses for the meetings of the commission are paid by the council that elected them.

Judicial commissions act on behalf of their electing bodies to try the cases brought before them. They are serving the functions of judge and jury in secular courts—they hear and decide questions of fact and interpret the "law" (Constitution) of the church when trying a case. If a judicial commission finds that an irregularity or a delinquency exists, it has the power to order the less-inclusive council or the Presbyterian Mission Agency or an agency of the General Assembly to correct its mistake or to do its duty. It can also order that body to "conduct further proceedings in the matter" [D-7.0402b]. If the commission finds that an offense has been committed by an individual, it can impose certain censures on the person (see section below on disciplinary cases). The decision of a case by a permanent judicial commission becomes the decision of the council that elected it. This means, for instance, that while the decision of a presbytery's judicial commission can be appealed to the synod, the presbytery itself cannot overturn the decision or set it aside.

In understanding how judicial process works in the Presbyterian system, it is helpful to know something about standing and jurisdiction, or who has authority to bring cases or to hear cases. Basically, in remedial cases standing is as follows [D-6.0202]: church members have standing to complain against the session to presbytery; sessions and members of presbytery have standing to complain to synod against their presbytery; also a council may complain against another council on the same level under the provisions of D-6.0202a(5).

When a case has been initiated, it is then heard by the appropriate council. Presbytery hears complaints against its sessions; synod hears complaints relating to presbyteries. The General Assembly hears complaints from members of synod against synod, complaints from presbyteries against synod, complaints from individuals who claim to have been injured by a General Assembly agency, and complaints from any less-inclusive council against the Presbyterian Mission Agency or an agency of the General Assembly. In disciplinary cases

> The session of a church has original jurisdiction . . . involving members of that church.

> The presbytery has original jurisdiction in disciplinary cases involving teaching elder members of that presbytery and ruling elders commissioned to pastoral service in congregations in the presbytery. [D-3.0101].

In rare cases, a council will give up its jurisdiction and pass the case on to the next higher council. This is called "reference" [D-4.0000]. A council may also lose its jurisdiction by its failure to act.

Remedial Cases. The process of correcting an error in the church through a remedial case begins with the filing of a complaint. Any member of a council at the time that an objectionable action has occurred can complain to the next higher council concerning that action. John Harper could complain to the synod, for example. Individual members of local churches can file complaints against their session but not against the actions of higher councils unless they are members of those bodies. (The exception to this rule is that employees of General Assembly entities who have suffered injury or damage to themselves or their property from the Presbyterian Mission Agency or a General Assembly agency can complain to the General Assembly.) Sessions, presbyteries, and synods can file complaints against the actions of the Presbyterian Mission Agency or one of the Assembly's agencies. The party bringing the complaint is called the complainant. The council being complained against is called the respondent.

A "complaint" is a written statement that contains basic information about the problem as outlined in D-6.0301. Complaints should be concise and specific. They must be filed within ninety days of the time that the error occurred or, in the case of a delinquency, of the refusal to act on the part of the respondent after written request. A copy of the complaint must be delivered to the respondent, and proof of delivery must accompany the filing of the complaint with the clerk of the more-inclusive council [D-6.0301f].

A party that is involved in judicial process, either as respondent or complainant, is represented before the more-inclusive council by a committee of no more than three persons, called the committee of counsel. They represent the party until the case is finally settled, including all appeals. The function of this committee is much like that of lawyers in secular courts. They defend or prosecute the case before the judicial commission. The *Book of Order* specifies that all parties in remedial and disciplinary cases are entitled to appear at trial and to be represented by professional attorneys, provided that all such attorneys must be members of the Presbyterian Church (U.S.A.).

After a complaint has been filed against a council, the Presbyterian Mission Agency, or a General Assembly agency, that body's committee of counsel must file an answer to the complaint with the stated clerk of the more-inclusive council within forty-five days, also sending a copy to the complainant. Contents of this answer are outlined in D-6.0303. Also within forty-five days, the clerk of the respondent council shall list in writing to the parties all the papers and other materials pertaining to the case [D-6.0307a]. The complainant has fifteen days to request that more materials be submitted. After notification by the stated clerk of the higher council of jurisdiction that the case has been accepted, the clerk of session or the stated clerk of the respondent must pass these materials on to the stated clerk of the more-inclusive council without delay. After the judicial commission has received the papers, the moderator and clerk of the permanent judicial commission must notify the parties that the materials are in its hands and give them an estimated date when the trial will be held. The judicial commission may also ask the parties to prepare and file briefs outlining their evidence and arguments, much as in the secular courts.

These comments are meant to give a brief overview of the procedures involved in a remedial case. They are in no way exhaustive; anyone who is involved in such a case should make a careful study of D-6.0000 and D-7.0000.

Disciplinary Cases. Cases involving the offenses of members against the Scriptures or our church's Constitution tend not to be as prevalent as remedial cases. However, there are times when the Rules of Discipline must be used to preserve the peace and purity of the church. Disciplinary cases could arise out of a conflict in the church, such as that at Clearview Presbyterian in our opening vignette. Open scandal in the church, damaging its reputation, could also call for disciplinary charges. Someone who feels that gossip is undermining his or her good name could use this process as a means of vindication. False teaching or heresy in the church may be corrected by disciplinary action.

Full instructions for this kind of case are found in D-10.0000 and D-11.0000, and those involved in disciplinary cases should take great care to conform to the procedures in these chapters. It should be noted that the *Book of Order* provides for time limitations on the filing of disciplinary charges. The exception to these rules on limitations is an accusation of sexual abuse against another person. Such charges may be brought no matter how long it has been since the offense is alleged to have taken place [D-10.0401b].

When an accusation has been made against an individual, a special disciplinary committee investigates the accusation to see if the evidence warrants the filing of official charges. This committee also prosecutes the charges before the judicial commission or session at all hearings and appeals. The prosecution in a disciplinary case is always a council of the church, even when the charge originated in one individual's accusation against another. It is the duty of the special disciplinary committee to work with the accused to see if the filing of charges can be avoided by use of alternative forms of resolution [D-10.0202i]. If the situation can be corrected in any other way, judicial process should not be used.

The accused person in a disciplinary case has rights similar to those of persons in secular criminal court proceedings: the right to remain silent, the right to call witnesses in his or her defense, the right to be represented by counsel, and the right to have counsel provided if the accused person is not able to afford it. Our system of church government makes a special effort to see that accused persons are treated fairly and given every chance to defend themselves.

If one is found guilty of an offense against the Scripture or the Constitution of the church, censures can be imposed against him or her. A censure is a kind of punishment. As outlined in D-12.0000, censures include rebuke (verbal criticism), rebuke with supervised rehabilitation, temporary exclusion from membership in the church or ordered ministry, and removal from ordered ministry or membership. Temporary exclusion is suspension from being a member or ordered minister for a limited period of time. In 1998, the Rules of Discipline added a fourth level of censure called "rebuke with supervised rehabilitation." This censure allows the council that has jurisdiction over the offender to order and oversee a process of rehabilitation while the person continues to hold and exercise leadership in the church. Specifics on this form of censure are found in D-12.0103. Removal from membership or ordered ministry is permanent unless the person is later restored as outlined in D-12.0200. One's ordination to ordered ministry is annulled and/or one's name is stricken from the rolls of the church.

Trials and Appeals

Detailed instructions for trials in remedial cases are found in D-7.0000 and for disciplinary cases in D-11.0000. These sections will be of special interest to sessions or permanent judicial commissions involved in hearing cases or to individuals who are bringing remedial complaints or defending themselves against disciplinary charges.

After a case has been heard and a verdict has been given, the verdict or decision can be appealed to the next more-inclusive council. Decisions of the permanent judicial commission of the General Assembly are final in all cases. In appeals, jurisdiction is as follows:

> Presbytery permanent judicial commissions hear appeals from disciplinary decisions of sessions, synod permanent judicial commissions hear appeals from the decisions of presbytery permanent judicial commissions in both remedial and disciplinary cases, . . . the General Assembly's permanent judicial commission hears appeals from remedial and disciplinary decisions of synod permanent judicial commissions [D-8.0000, D-13.0000].

All appeals are heard and decided by permanent judicial commissions. Their task is to review the way the case was handled by the lower commission or session and to make sure that the proceedings were fair and correct according to the Constitution. The commission that hears an appeal has the power to "correct, modify, set aside, or reverse" the proceedings and judgment of the less-inclusive body [D-8.0101, D-13.0100]. Only those people or councils who were first involved in the case, the original parties, are eligible to appeal the decision to a more-inclusive council.

Written notice of appeal must be filed and received by the clerk of the council that elected the permanent judicial commission whose decision is being complained against within forty-five days after the decision is delivered to the parties. The content of this notice of appeal is listed in D-8.0202 and D-13.0202. It is very important to observe the deadlines given for complaints and appeals and for the filing of all necessary papers in a judicial case; to miss a deadline is to risk having the case or appeal dismissed.

The judicial commission hearing an appeal is not to retry the case. It does not go back and hear the evidence again in order to make its own decision on the facts. The job of the commission is to decide whether the proceedings were fair and were carried out according to the Constitution of the church. Grounds for appeal as listed in the Rules of Discipline [D-8.0105] include the following:

a. Irregularity in the proceedings;
b. Refusing a party reasonable opportunity to be heard or to obtain or present evidence;
c. Receiving improper, or declining to receive proper, evidence or testimony;
d. Hastening to a decision before the evidence or testimony is fully received;
e. Manifestation of prejudice in the conduct of the case;
f. Injustice in the process or decision;
g. Error in constitutional interpretation.

Stay of Enforcement. If a decision of a council or the Presbyterian Mission Agency or an agency or the verdict of a judicial commission is being appealed or complained of to a more-inclusive body, anyone who is eligible to appeal or complain can keep the decision from being carried out until the appeal or complaint has been decided finally. The means for this is called a "stay of enforcement" [D-6.0103]. In the example at the beginning of the chapter, by filing such a stay John Harper could have prevented the candidate from being ordained and installed until a complaint on the matter could be heard by the synod. Basically, a stay of enforcement holds everything "as is," until an appeal can be filed and heard. There are three ways to get a stay of enforcement. For a stay against the action of a council, the signatures of at least one-third of the members of the body who were recorded as present when the objectionable action was taken are required. To get a stay of enforcement against the decision of a permanent judicial commission, one-third of the members who decided the case must sign.

Another alternative is to have three members of the judicial commission to which the action or decision would be appealed certify that in their opinion there are grounds for upholding a complaint against the decision or action and that it may have been in error. In order to certify this, they must have in hand a complaint or the substance of a complaint that is to be filed. A stay of enforcement is in effect until the time has run out for filing a complaint or appeal or until the matter has been decided by the permanent judicial commission that has jurisdiction.

Our system of church government recognizes that conflict may occur even within the Christian community, and it gives us the means to deal with it fairly and efficiently. If wisely used, the Rules of Discipline can do much to preserve the peace and purity of the church.

Questions for Reflection and Discussion

1. When was the last time your congregation had a conflict? How was it handled? What was learned through the experience? Was anything clarified through the conflict regarding the congregation's mission, programs, or values?

2. What is your normal reaction to conflict? Fight? Flight? Freeze? Some other?

3. Have you ever seen anyone lodge a dissent or protest in a council meeting? How was it received?

4. Is discipline the same as punishment? If they are different, what makes the difference?

Chapter Fourteen

LEADING
THE CHURCH
IN WORSHIP

John Dowler, chair of the worship committee at Sunshine Presbyterian Church, was changing the paraments before worship one Sunday morning when he was cornered by an angry church member. Waving the worship bulletin in John's face, the member all but shouted, "I am sick and tired of these awful hymns we sing every Sunday! Ever since that music director came, we have not sung a hymn I recognize, and I've been a Presbyterian all my life. Who's in charge of picking the hymns for the service? And why can't those of us in the pew have something to say about what we sing?"

The regular monthly session meeting of the Downtown Presbyterian Church was drawing to a close when a ruling elder rose to present a piece of business. "I have gotten several calls this week," he began, "about the guest preacher we had last Sunday. A number of people were very upset by what she said about capital punishment. In fact, the members of one family were so angry they were talking about leaving the church! I would like to make a motion that in the future all guest preachers and the topics of their messages must be approved by the session before they are invited to fill our pulpit." Several other ruling elders nodded approvingly, but one session member turned to the pastor and said, "Does the *Book of Order* give us the power to do this?"

The Directory for Worship

Even before the United Presbyterian Church in the United States of America and the Presbyterian Church in the United States reunited in 1983, groups in both churches were working on various parts of a new directory for worship. After reunion, a task force was created to pull these efforts together and incorporate them into a comprehensive guide for Presbyterian worship.

In 1985 the task force to write a new directory for worship made public the principles that would guide their work. They stated that the new directory would:

1. Reflect Biblical understandings of the human response to God's presence and action in the life of the world
2. Be guided by the faith and practice of the church through the ages
3. Be guided by that heritage which frees us to resist imposed forms but constrains us to obey God's Word in matters of worship
4. Be informed by our Reformed confessions
5. Be in scope and orientation catholic [universal] rather than sectarian
6. Be open to the richness of traditional and cultural ways of responding to God's grace
7. Assure an openness to the Holy Spirit's creativity, which is spontaneous yet orderly
8. Emphasize worship as the work of all the people, whose different gifts are expressed through different functions and ministries
9. Recognize that as we faithfully worship God, the Holy Spirit calls and sends us to bear witness to Jesus Christ in the world through grateful and obedient service, and
10. Be the product of reflection, debate, and consideration by the whole church.

The Directory for Worship, after approval by the General Assembly of 1988, was sent out to the presbyteries. A majority of the presbyteries must vote in favor of any proposed change in the *Book of Order* before it goes into effect. After receiving affirmative votes by a large majority of the presbyteries, the Directory was published in the 1989–90 edition of the *Book of Order*. It is part of the standards of our church. It contains the theology and polity that shape the worship and ministry of the church. It is not, however, a service book, with detailed instructions for actual services of worship, or a prayer book. True to our "free church" tradition, the Directory for Worship lays the foundation and draws the outlines for worship in the church without prescribing liturgies. It does not contain required prayers or rituals. Such tools with which to build on the Directory's foundation can be found in the *Book of Common Worship* published by our denomination.

There is a distinctive emphasis in the Directory for Worship that merits notice: It recognizes and makes allowances for the diversity of the church. The Presbyterian Church (U.S.A.) contains all kinds of congregations, some large and some small, some considering themselves theologically liberal and some who see themselves as conservative, some with a large, trained staff, and some with no paid staff persons. Churches also differ according to the part of the country in which they are located and according to the racial or ethnic backgrounds of their members. The Directory attempts to leave room for all kinds of churches to build a worship life that meets their needs while being faithful to the Reformed tradition.

What Is Worship?

When God touches our lives, we feel the call to worship. Worship is a response to the experience of the presence of God in our midst. The gathered people of God worship in answer to the call of God that brings them into existence. God is both the creator and the object of our worship. Without the Spirit of God moving among us, worship is impossible. Worship occurs whenever we respond to God with praise, repentance, obedience, and service.

The experience of worship never leaves us unmoved or unchanged. It impacts the will as well as the mind and the emotions. "The Spirit of God quickens people to an awareness of God's grace and claim upon their lives. The Spirit moves them to respond by naming and calling upon God, by remembering and proclaiming God's acts of self-revelation in word and deed, and by committing their lives to God's reign in the world" [W-1.1002a].

The Directory for Worship points to the life of Jesus as the perfect human response to God. Jesus' whole life was an offering of worship. His obedience to God, his healing presence, his inspired teaching, his service to those in need, and his sacrifice for our sin on the cross all illustrate an existence perfectly focused on the divine reality. "Jesus Christ is the living God present in common life" [W-1.1003c]. The story of Jesus bears out the truth that worship is not something separate from everyday life; worship is life.

The Elements of Worship

The Directory identifies six essential elements of worship in the Christian community [W-2.0000]. All these elements may not be present in each worship experience; yet, taken together, they form the fabric of the church's worship life.

Prayer. Listening to God and speaking to God are at the center of the Christian life and, therefore, at the center of worship. While prayer may commonly include expressions of adoration, thanksgiving, confession, intercession, and petition, no expression of honest human thought or feeling is inappropriate for prayer. Prayer can reflect doubts and struggles of faith. It can involve an offering of self and possessions. Prayer may take the form of an act of commitment to God's will. Even the anger and pain of the

people of God can be lifted up in the form of a lam
is perfect love of God and perfect obedience to God
    The Directory draws music into the context of pra
faithful in common prayer wherever they gather for
church, home, or other special place" [W-2.1003]. Thu
be used in worship to entertain. The aesthetics of music
the service of the purpose of worship: to draw us close   ...u nelp
us to respond to God's grace and demands.

    In order to experience the fullness of prayer, worship contains prayer-
ful actions as well as speech and song. In worship, "it is appropriate," the
Directory states,

    a. to kneel, to bow, to stand, to lift hands in prayer,
    b. to dance, to clap [but not applaud as at a performance!], to embrace
        in joy and praise,
    c. to anoint and to lay on hands in intercession and supplication,
        commissioning and ordination. [W-2.1005]

Scripture Read and Proclaimed. If prayer is at the heart of worship, Scripture
is its lifeblood. Scripture is the Word of God in written form. The Directory for Worship states that "where that Word is read and proclaimed,
Jesus Christ the Living Word is present by the inward witness of the Holy
Spirit" [W-2.2001].

    It is the duty of the session to ensure that Scripture is read and pro-
claimed regularly to the congregation in a language that the people can
understand. It is the responsibility of the teaching elder to select the
Scripture to be read, making sure that a wide range of biblical readings are
covered over the course of time. The pastor or person invited to preach also
selects the version of Scripture to be read.

    The Directory does not limit the proclamation of the Word to preach-
ing and the reading of Scripture. Creeds and confessions are also ways
to hear and express response to the Scriptures. Other creative possibilities for proclaiming the Word include appropriate dramas, video
presentations, storytelling, cantatas, oratorios and anthems, hymns,
spirituals, other songs, and liturgical dance. If these means of setting
forth the message of Scripture are used, care shall be taken to make sure
that the gospel message is clearly expressed in ways that are appropriate to worship.

Baptism and the Lord's Supper. The sacraments could be called the gospel in
active form. The session bears significant responsibility in seeing that both
sacraments are offered to the congregation. A full discussion of baptism
and the Lord's Supper follows under the section "The Font and the Table,"
on page 151.

-offering. The emphasis on the offering of one's self as an act of worship is a distinctive facet of the Directory. Self-offering includes, but goes far beyond, the giving of money and/or possessions. In fact, the Directory declares that the whole "Christian life is an offering of one's self to God" [W-2.5001].

The giving of material offerings in the context of a service of worship is an act of self-dedication by the whole worshiping community. This is why the most meaningful and appropriate way to receive the offerings of the people is to gather them during the service of worship. It is unfortunate that in an attempt to make giving easy some congregations have chosen to use automatic deductions from bank accounts and credit cards as their major way of receiving offerings. These methods strip the offering of its powerful liturgical meanings.

Along with the offering of material gifts of the people, worship should also include opportunities for people to dedicate themselves to the mission of the church in the world. Presentations such as the Minute for Mission and special worship emphases throughout the year hold faith and works together before the people. Worship should include invitations to deepen discipleship, to join the church, and to make a commitment to particular Christian ministries.

Relating to Each Other and the World. We do not worship in isolation. Even when one worships alone, one is bound up in the mystic communion of the worshiping saints of all times and places. Times in the service of worship that are particularly appropriate for expressing our concern for each other include the gathering at the beginning of worship, during the confession and after the declaration of pardon, in times of greeting during the service, and in preparation for the prayers of the people. We can also share and support our individual and common ministries during worship, giving witness to the work of the church in the world.

The Order of Worship

Presbyterians do not have prayer books with required prayers or liturgies; in this sense we fall into what has historically been known as the "free church" tradition. The Presbyterian way of structuring the service of worship does strive to be faithful to the witness of Scripture. Outside the Scriptures, however, there is no absolute standard governing the ordering of services.

The Directory offers a suggested rationale for the ordering of worship that takes Scripture, contemporary needs, and the traditions of the church into account. All the parts of congregational worship on the Lord's Day are presented in terms of five actions relating to the Scripture [W-3.3202]:

1. Gathering around the Word
2. Proclaiming the Word
3. Responding to the Word
4. The sealing of the Word (sacraments)
5. Bearing and following the Word into the world

The Directory contains helpful suggestions as to specific elements of worship appropriate for each of these parts of the service.

While placing primary emphasis on the Service for the Lord's Day, the Directory also discusses the ordering of worship at other times [W-3.4001–.6205]. These occasions include daily prayer, services on Sunday other than in the morning, worship in the church school, prayer meetings, services of prayer for healing, services for evangelism, times of mission emphasis, and other regular meetings of church groups. Council meetings, retreats, camps, and conference centers are also the setting for very significant worship experiences. If worship is held in a setting other than the Service for the Lord's Day (especially if Communion is involved), the council having jurisdiction over those involved in the gathering shall authorize it and take note that it is ordered in an appropriate way.

The Context of Worship

Another distinctive feature of this Directory is that it pays special attention to the setting of worship. Beginning with the subject of time, the Directory says that while "Christians may worship at any time. . . . God set aside one day in seven to be kept holy" [W-1.3011(1)]. This day (usually Sunday, in celebration of the resurrection of Jesus) is known as the Lord's Day. The Directory also commends daily public worship as an expression of our Reformed heritage and of our roots in the Jewish worship tradition.

Just as the time of worship is not essential to its nature, neither is a particular space necessary for worship. Worship happens wherever believers commune with their risen Lord. Whatever space is used for worship, it should be arranged in such a way that it promotes ease of gathering for all people, a sense of being in community, and an openness to the presence of God, who is holy. The place should contain furnishings for the sacraments of baptism and the Lord's Supper. The close relationship between Word and sacraments suggests that the font and table should be near the place where Scripture is read and preached.

While we worship a God whose nature is spiritual, we must never forget that this God created our world and called it good, and that God also became incarnate in Jesus Christ. We believe that the created world belongs to God and reflects God's glory. Therefore, the spiritual and the material are closely intertwined in worship. The Old Testament tells of the use of "Ark, showbread, woven and embroidered linens, basins, oil, lights, musical instruments, grain, fruit, and animals" to worship and praise God [W-1.3031]. Jesus himself made use of physical objects in his ministry. We remember his taking water and a towel to wash the disciples' feet. We remember his breaking bread and pouring wine. We remember his parables about trees, pearls, coins, and sheep. We remember that he accepted worship in the form of a jar of ointment poured over his body.

The worship of the early church gave prominence to three physical elements as signs of the gospel: water, wine, and bread. We are heirs of this sacramental tradition. We believe that these material things as they are used in worship express the gospel in physical form. "Sacraments are signs of the real presence and power of Christ in the Church, symbols of God's action. Through the Sacraments, God seals believers in redemption, renews their identity as the people of God, and marks them for service" [W-1.3033(2)].

Along with the sacraments, worship is enriched by the creative offerings of the people of God. These might include artwork, vestments, sanctuary furnishings and accessories, banners, preaching, vocal and instrumental music, drama, and dance. Even the architecture of the buildings and rooms used by the congregation can be an offering of worship to God [W-1.3034]. In all these things, care shall be taken to see that the focus remains on God and not on the offerings or those making them.

Along with time, space, and matter, language is an essential element of worship. Worship takes place within the context of the Word. The speaking, hearing, and understanding of the Word are crucial to drawing us closer to God and to our neighbors. The Directory gives considerable attention to the place of language in worship.

First, it is important to understand how symbols are used in the language of the church. Two realities are held in tension here: on the one hand, no human symbol can express the fullness of God's being; on the other hand, because of the limitations of our human nature we must use symbols to talk about God. Symbolic language and actions used in worship are acceptable and useful as long as they point to the reality of God expressed in the life, death, and resurrection of Jesus [W-1.2002].

When we talk about God as the Rock of Ages, for instance, we know that God is not really a rock. But there is something about the solidness and the enduring qualities of a rock that remind us of God's faithfulness. When we use masculine or feminine words to talk about God, we are not saying that God is either physically male or female, but rather that the qualities we find often in men or in women remind us of how God acts toward us.

Along with the use of symbols, the Directory raises the issue of using appropriate language in worship. Such language

a. is more expressive than rationalistic,
b. builds up and persuades as well as informs and describes,
c. creates ardor as well as order,
d. is the utterance of the whole community of faith as well as the devotion of individuals. [W-1.2005]

The inclusive nature of the gospel also requires that the language of worship be language that does not exclude people on the basis of such things as gender or race.

The Font and the Table

Baptism. This sacrament is "the sign and seal of incorporation into Christ" [W-2.3001]. In baptism we

> participate in Jesus' death and resurrection [W-2.3002],
> die to what separates us from God and are raised to newness of life [W-2.3002],
> are bound, with the whole church, in covenant to our Creator and Lord [W-2.3003],
> are united with the people of God of every place and time in a way that calls all barriers between individuals and peoples into question [W-2.3005],
> receive our identity as God's people and our commission for service [W-2.3006].

"Baptism enacts and seals what the Word proclaims: God's redeeming grace offered to all people" [W-2.3006].

In the Presbyterian Church we baptize people one time only. It is true that persons baptized as infants or children may have no conscious memory of their baptism. However, the effectiveness of baptism does not depend on our memory or appreciation of it at the time of its administration. Later experiences of conversion or spiritual growth do not invalidate our earlier baptism; instead these experiences are the natural fruit of baptism. "Baptism signifies the beginning of life in Christ, not its completion" [W-2.3007].

While the Directory emphatically denies the possibility of a person's being baptized more than once, it does encourage all baptized Christians to renew their baptism frequently. This involves a recommitment to Christ and to his service. Renewal of baptismal promises can take place each time we see another baptized and each time we celebrate the Lord's Supper. Suggestions for a more formal renewal of baptism can be found in the *Book of Common Worship.*

In our churches we baptize infants, children, and adults. Whatever the age of the person being baptized, the sacrament is the same. However, with adults the symbolism focuses on our decision to follow Jesus and our response in faithfulness to God's gracious call. With children and babies the symbolic emphasis is on the unconditional grace that claims us before we know anything about it or can respond in any way. Whether persons have been baptized as adults or as children, our denomination recognizes as valid all Christian baptisms with water in the name of the Trinity.

The form of baptism does not affect its validity, although each of the three commonly used methods has a different symbolic thrust. Pouring water over the one to be baptized reminds us of the pouring out of the Holy Spirit at Pentecost. Sprinkling reminds us of the cleansing power of the blood of Jesus. Immersion reminds us that through faith we have died with Christ and have been raised to walk in newness of life.

While a teaching elder or commissioned ruling elder always does the actual baptizing, the Directory for Worship places primary responsibility for baptism in the hands of (1) the session, (2) the congregation, and (3) the parents of children being baptized [W-2.3014]. The session (of which the pastor is a member) bears the responsibility to see that parents are encouraged to present their children for baptism at the appropriate time. We do not believe that children who die unbaptized go to hell or to limbo; therefore, we do not rush to baptize children immediately after birth. However, delaying baptism of children is discouraged. The session also is responsible to instruct and examine those adults who desire to be baptized upon profession of their faith. After the baptism the session will enter the baptized persons on the appropriate rolls of the church and make sure that the newly baptized persons and the parents who may have presented them for baptism are nurtured and encouraged in the life of faith [W-2.3012].

The congregation bears the responsibility to do the actual nurturing in the faith, to draw the baptized into the church family, and to make sure that they have all things necessary for growth in the faith. Special responsibilities in this area may be delegated to persons such as church school teachers, children's workers, and sponsors appointed by the session [W-2.3013].

The parents who are presenting children for baptism ordinarily are active members of the congregation. Members other than parents may also present children for baptism if they exercise parental responsibility for them. Sessions may choose to allow parents who are active members of another congregation to present children for baptism, but they are not required to do so.

The Directory also provides for baptism under unusual circumstances outside the normal worship of the congregation. The celebration of baptism may be authorized, for example, by chaplains or others engaged in ordered ministries serving in "hospitals, prisons, schools, or other institutions," armed forces, and new church developments [W-2.3011b]. However, in all such cases the baptism must be entered in the records of some congregation.

In W-3.3602–.3608 the Directory gives detailed suggestions and instructions as to the ordering of the baptismal service. It is most important to note that the sacrament shall be set in the context of reading and proclaiming of the Word. This must be done in such a way that the meaning of baptism will be understood and the responsibilities of candidates for baptism, parents presenting children for baptism, session, and congregation will be made clear.

The Lord's Supper. If baptism is the sign and seal of our entry into the community of faith by grace, the Lord's Supper is the sign and seal of our continued experience of this renewing grace. In Communion we

> give thanks to God;
> remember the life, death, and resurrection of Jesus;
> anticipate the coming of God's Kingdom in all its fullness, and offer ourselves to work toward the day when God's will shall be done on earth as it is in heaven;
> are nourished in our faith and strengthened in our commitment;
> call on the Holy Spirit to be present among us in power and join in "communion with Christ and with all who belong to Christ" [W-2.4003–.4006].

Because of this communion, all faithful, baptized persons are welcome at the Lord's Table in a Presbyterian church, regardless of their denomination or any other human condition. The invitation is extended to baptized children who are being nurtured in the faith as well as to confirmed believers.

The Directory states that it is appropriate to observe Communion in worship as frequently as every Sunday. A minimum of once a quarter is required [W-2.4012a]. The best situation is for Communion to be celebrated often enough so that it seems like a normal part of the congregation's worship, not an unusual event.

While Communion is generally celebrated during public worship, the Directory also specifies that "the Lord's Supper may be observed in connection with the visitation of the sick and those isolated from public worship as a means of extending the church's ministry to them" [W-2.4010]. In the same way that the Word is always read and proclaimed when Communion is celebrated in public worship, so is it when the Lord's Table is laid in the sick room or living room. In order to show forth the communion of the saints and the unity of the body of Christ in these special circumstances, the teaching elder shall be accompanied by one or more church members authorized by the session to represent the congregation [W-2.4010]. A session or council always authorizes the celebration of the Lord's Supper. A group wishing to observe the sacrament shall seek the permission of the council having jurisdiction over that group. For instance, if the Presbyterian Women of a particular church want to celebrate Communion at a retreat, the session would be requested to authorize it. If a presbytery youth council wanted to have Communion at the close of its youth rally, presbytery would be requested to authorize the sacrament.

In W-3.3609 and following, instructions for the ordering of Communion are given. This section mandates that at least one week's notice be given before Communion in order to allow for personal and communal preparation for the sacrament. First Corinthians 11:23–26 or one of its Gospel parallels is specified for use during the breaking of the bread and pouring of the cup or in the Prayer of Thanksgiving. No particular way of distributing the elements is mandated, but a number of possibilities are mentioned. The session is responsible for deciding what form of grape product will be used in Communion; if wine is used, however, unfermented grape juice must also be provided and clearly identified as such.

Worship on Special Occasions

Although the Word and Sacraments are always the focus of Christian worship, Chapter IV of the Directory deals with nine special circumstances that bear recognition in the life of the congregation and individuals. A number of these occasions, such as receiving new members, welcoming children to the Lord's Table, welcoming new members into the church, renewal of baptism and other commitments, and commissioning for service in the church and world are generally incorporated into the Service for the Lord's Day. Also in this category might be included the marking of transitions in ministry; the recognition of one or more members' service outside the church; the ordination and installation of ruling elders, deacons, and teaching elders; services expressing repentance and reconciliation; and services imposing the censures of the church [see D-12.0000].

Two special occasions for worship are dealt with at greater length. These are services at the time of marriage and of death. The Directory states that "as a service of Christian worship, the marriage service is under the direction of the teaching elder and the supervision of the session" [W-4.9003]. All things relating to the service, including music and decorations, should reflect its character as a service of worship. When Communion is celebrated along with the marriage service, it requires authorization by the session. All baptized persons present must be invited to partake of the sacrament.

The section on funerals specifies that ordinarily the service will be held in the church "in order to join this service to the community's continuing life and witness to the resurrection" [W-4.10003]. The teaching elder is in charge of this service. The Christian service of worship takes precedence over fraternal or other rites, which should be conducted separately from worship. Whatever the specifics of the service, the focus should be on the hope of resurrection that Christians share in Christ and the comforting of those who grieve [W-4.10001].

Worship and Personal Discipleship

The Directory for Worship not only gives instructions for ordering the worship life of the congregation but also offers help in developing rich worship experiences for individuals, families, and small groups. Worship is never private. Even when we worship by ourselves, we are still bound up in the communion of the saints that transcends all limits of time and space. One who is committed to growing in the faith will make time during the day for worship, either alone or with small groups of other believers. This is part of being a disciple of Christ: to take advantage of the means of grace that God has placed at our disposal. The more we commit ourselves to ministry and serious discipleship, the more we will need frequent worship and sacraments.

The Directory says that daily personal worship may take place when we are assembled in groups, in households and families, or in solitude [W-5.2001]. The emphasis is on "finding the times and places where one can focus on God's presence, hear God's Word, and respond to God's grace in prayer, self-offering, and commitment to service" [W-5.2001]. The key elements of daily personal worship are Scripture and prayer. The Directory reminds us that "one may read Scripture for . . . guidance, support, comfort, encouragement, and challenge" [W-5.3002a]. Study of the Scriptures as historical and literary documents is commended. Other ways to encounter Scripture include meditation, memorization, reflection, and praying the Scriptures. Using imagination to enter into the world of the original hearers is another helpful method of approaching Scripture. When we are confronted with the challenges of the Word, we may find ourselves wrestling with its demands and being led to offer ourselves in obedience to God in response [W-5.3002]. The use of a journal in the study of Scripture is recommended, along with some kind of systematic tool, such as a lectionary, for covering the whole message of the Scriptures.

Prayer is another essential part of the discipline of personal worship. Prayer can take many forms, and one committed to Christian growth will do well to explore a wide variety of such forms. The Directory lists a number of possibilities, including conversation with God, waiting before God in silence, meditation, communion with God beyond words, praying in tongues, and acting out prayer in various kinds of movement. What is commonly called intercessory prayer is commended, and we are encouraged to hold the events and peoples of the world, as well as those close to us, before God. Prayer is learned through the discipline of praying, and the use of a wide variety of aids, such as Scripture, prayer books, hymnals, and literature and visual art, is helpful in prayer education.

Other disciplines commended by the Directory are the keeping of the Lord's Day, public worship, cultivating the habits of rest and recreation, and taking part in ministry in Christ's name [W-5.5001]. Acts of fasting and keeping vigils (not sleeping, in order to pray through the night) may also be helpful means of personal discipleship related to prayer. Any serious disciple will sooner or later be brought to deal with issues of stewardship in his or her life. The use of property in the name of God is an important facet of discipleship. "Tithing is a primary expression of the Christian discipline of stewardship. . . . Those who follow the discipline of Christian stewardship will find themselves called to lives of simplicity, generosity, honesty, hospitality, compassion, receptivity, and concern for the earth and God's creatures" [W-5.5004–.5005].

Worship and Ministry

Worship of the true God never leaves the worshiper unchanged. Those who truly worship will be drawn into the service of God. The Directory for Worship talks about the various ministries of the people of God, dividing them into those carried out within the community of faith and those carried out in the world.

The church is engaged in a number of activities aimed at meeting the needs of its members. The Directory speaks of these in terms of nurture and pastoral care. Nurture includes the cultivation of faith in persons at all stages of their life, from baptism to the deathbed. The nurture of the church prepares persons for baptism, leads them to a profession of Jesus Christ as Lord and Savior, and gives them training and resources to enable them to live as disciples of Christ in ministry to the world [W-6.2001].

The issue of vocation is mentioned several times in the Directory, especially in terms of the church's duty to guide, support, and provide resources for those who are living active lives of witness in the world. The idea that worship and the service of God in the world are inseparable is stressed. Therefore, the church bears the responsibility of connecting the worship life of the congregation with the vocation of Christians to serve God at home and in the school, workplace, neighborhood, nation, and world [W-6.2003].

The various stages of human life, and the losses and challenges connected with these stages, also offer opportunities for growth in faith. The Directory has a section on the ministry of pastoral care as an aid to such growth. Occasions such as illnesses, death, grief, loss of employment, divorce or separation, and children leaving home are mentioned as important times for pastoral care. The church often shies away from getting involved in delicate situations involving broken relationships and sin, but the power of the gospel extends especially to these situations. A congregation that wishes to minister to people in the whole of life will find sensitive ways of being present even to those caught up in painful circumstances [W-6.3008–.3009]. Such care might involve prayer, sacraments, and the sharing of Scripture and of familiar parts of the service of worship such as the Lord's Prayer, creeds, and psalms [W-6.3011].

The Directory concludes with a chapter on the ministry of the church in the world. Worship is closely linked with serving God's purposes in the world because "worship presents the reality of the divine rule which God has promised in Jesus Christ" [W-7.1001]. Worship and mission feed each other. In worship we are called into mission; as we engage in mission we find ourselves ever returning to God with our praise and our need for renewal.

The ministry of the church in the world has a number of facets. Proclamation of the Word and sharing the good news are placed in the context of worship, where the Word is regularly read and proclaimed. In worship, ministries of compassion to persons in need are encouraged "as the faithful respond in prayers of confession and intercession, in acts of self-offering, and in offering material goods" to be used in these ministries [W-7.3002]. Another facet of the church's mission in the world involves working for peace and justice. This is a ministry of reconciliation that draws on the Scriptures' call for holiness and justice in our personal dealings with others and in our larger society. The stewardship of life and creation is another facet of the mission of God's people. In worship, our thanksgiving is coupled with commitment to live on the earth in ways that glorify God and do not tend toward destruction.

All these ministries are called forth and empowered by the Holy Spirit, whose presence enables all the ministry and worship of the church. Through the presence and working of the Spirit "the Church's ministries of evangelism and caring for creation, of compassion and reconciliation are signs of God's reign and offer hope in the midst of life-denying situations. That hope is not dependent on the success of the Church's ministries or the effectiveness of its worship, but is sustained by the power of God present with the Church as it ministers and worships" [W-7.6002]. Quite appropriately, the Directory ends with a statement of hope for the coming of the reign of God (Phil. 2:9–11) and ascriptions of praise to God (Jude 24 and Rev. 7:12).

Responsibilities for Worship

It is the duty of the session in each church to make sure both that opportunities to worship are made available to the congregation and that people are encouraged to take full advantage of these opportunities. The Directory places oversight of the worship of the congregation squarely in the hands of the session [W-1.4004].

Specifically, the session is responsible to see that the

a. preaching of the Word,
b. celebration of the Sacraments,
c. corporate prayer, and
d. offering of praise to God in song

occur regularly in the congregation [W-1.4004]. In this regard, the session is authorized

e. to oversee and approve all public worship in the life of the particular church with the exception of those responsibilities delegated to the teaching elder alone [W-1.4005]
f. to determine occasions, days, times, and places for worship [W-1.4004].

The Directory also gives the session direct responsibility to determine where worship shall be held and how the space is to be arranged and furnished. This responsibility includes exercising its discretion about the use of flowers, banners, candles, and other such things in worship. The music program of the church, as well as other activities involving the arts, are under the oversight of the session. The session also supervises the persons who are involved in leading worship "through music, drama, dance, and other arts" [W-1.4004j].

There are two duties mentioned in the Directory [W-1.4006] that the session and pastor share. Primary responsibility for deciding the order of worship lies with the pastor, but this shall be done in consultation with and with the agreement of the session. Primary responsibility for the choice of pew Bibles, hymnals, and other such aids to worship lies with the session, but they must consult with and secure the concurrence of the pastor. In choosing these worship aids, the Directory also specifies that other persons involved in leading the congregation (such as educators and church musicians) should also be consulted.

The second vignette at the beginning of this chapter raises the question of whether the session has the right to approve guest preachers. This is another area of worship planning in which the pastor and the session must work with each other. The Directory specifies that "a teaching elder or other person authorized by presbytery may be invited by the pastor with the concurrence of the session or, when there is no pastor, by the session" [W-2.2007]. This means that the pastor and the session must come to agreement before a particular person is invited.

The teaching elder of the congregation has certain duties in connection with choosing the contents of services of worship that "are not subject to the authority of the session" [W-1.4005]. These include

1. the selection of Scripture lessons to be read,
2. the preparation and preaching of the sermon or exposition of the Word,
3. the prayers offered on behalf of the people and those prepared for the use of the people in worship,
4. the music to be sung,
5. the use of drama, dance, and other art forms. [W-1.4005]

A wise teaching elder will confer with the session, other professionals on the church staff, and, if possible, a worship committee as she or he makes these important choices in the planning of worship.

Because of the emotional connections people have with familiar hymns, choosing hymns to be sung in worship is a particularly sensitive area of pastoral responsibility. In the first vignette at the beginning of the chapter, John Dowler could have explained to the irate church member that the pastor is responsible for the music sung in worship. He could then have suggested to the member that he share his concern about the hymns with the pastor. Perhaps the pastor should consult with the session and members of the congregation to see if the irate member's concern is generally shared. If so, he or she might consult with the music director on this matter, making the congregation's preferences known. If the pastor has delegated the selection of hymns entirely to the music staff, he or she might want to consider taking a more active role in this part of planning the congregation's worship.

By far the largest part of the responsibility for the congregation's worship lies with the session. Aside from the general oversight of the congregation's worship and its specific duties as discussed above, the session is also charged with providing worship education for the congregation. This shall be done for different age groups in ways that are appropriate to them. Worship is something we learn how to do. Therefore, learning to participate fully in worship is an important part of Christian education for persons of all ages. Along with this general education for worship, the Directory specifies that it shall be used as a regular part of the training of leaders of the church.

Following is a reference chart showing the places in the Directory where the session is mentioned in connection with worship.[1]

Accountability to presbytery for congregation's worship	W-1.4008
Authorizing services of worship other than the Service for the Lord's Day	
Daily prayer	W-3.4005
On Sunday	W-3.5101
Prayer meetings	W-3.5301
Services for wholeness	W-3.5402
Services for evangelism	W-3.5501
Services for mission interpretation	W-3.5601
Services for special groups in the congregation	W-3.5701
Baptism	
General responsibilities	W-2.3012
In extraordinary circumstances	W-2.3011a
Of children whose parents are not members of the congregation	W-2.3014
Children and worship	W-3.1004
Counsel about manifestations of the Spirit	W-3.1002b
Discipline of personal worship, encouraging	W-5.1004
Education for worship	W-1.4007
Encourage the people to participate fully in worship	W-1.4004
Guest preachers, concurrence, in teaching elder's invitation to	W-2.2007
Lord's Supper	
Authorizing the sacrament	W-2.4012a
Regular and frequent celebration of the sacrament	W-3.3101
Authorizing at retreats, etc.	W-3.6204
Services on the occasion of death (funerals)	W-4.10003
Manner of distribution decided by session	W-3.3616
On occasions other than worship on the Lord's Day	W-2.4010
Use of wine at Communion	W-3.3611
Welcoming children to the Lord's Table	W-4.2002
Marriage services	
Under the supervision of session	W-4.9003
If requested, counsel with minister on decision not to marry a couple	W-4.9002b
Meetings of pastor and choir director, responsibility to see that they occur regularly	W-1.4005(b)
Nurture	
Approval of resources	W-6.2006
Responsibility for educational program	W-6.2005

Ordering worship on the Lord's Day	W-3.3201
Provide for reading and preaching of the Word	W-2.2007
	W-2.2001
Reception of new members	W-4.2003
	W-4.2004
Sense of personal renewal shared with session	W-4.2006
Services on occasion of death	W-4.10002
Worship at session meetings	W-3.6101

The worship of the triune God is at the core of the church's identity. A church without worship is a church without life. Therefore, the session's responsibilities to encourage, nurture, and order the worship of the congregation are among the most important given to it by the *Book of Order.*

Questions for Reflection and Discussion

1. In your opinion, what is it that God wants to see when a congregation gathers for worship?

2. How does your church help homebound persons participate in the congregation's worship life?

3. Who plans worship in your congregation? Is the congregation ever given opportunities to critique their worship experience?

4. How does the session carry out its responsibilities for worship in your church?

NOTES

Chapter 1. A Polity for the Church

1. Stuart R. Oglesby, *Presbyterianism in Action* (Richmond: John Knox Press, 1949), pp. 34, 35.
2. Ben Lacy Rose, *Confirming Your Call* (Richmond: John Knox Press, 1967), p. 27.
3. Ibid., p. 19.

Chapter 2. Calling to Leadership in the Church

1. Robert Clyde Johnson, ed., *The Church and Its Changing Ministry* (Philadelphia: Office of the General Assembly, The United Presbyterian Church in the United States of America, 1961), p. 26.
2. Minutes, General Assembly, 2008.
3. When this edition of *Presbyterian Polity for Church Leaders* was created, the denomination had been living into G-2.0104b for only a few months. Many questions remain unanswered as to how it will be interpreted and administered. With the rest of the church we await further developments.
4. "Ordination to the Ministry of the Word" (Atlanta: Office of the Stated Clerk, Presbyterian Church in the United States, 1976), p. 6.
5. Robert W. Henderson, "Concerning the Eldership," *Reformed World* 1 (December 1973): p. 365.

Chapter 4. The Ordered Ministry of Ruling Elder

1. Janet G. MacGregor, *The Scottish Presbyterian Polity* (Edinburgh: Oliver and Boyd, 1926), p. xiv.
2. Ibid., p. xvi.
3. Ibid., p. 51.
4. Ibid.
5. Ibid., p. 112.
6. Ibid., p. 122.
7. Ernest Trice Thompson, *Presbyterians in the South* (Richmond: John Knox Press, 1963), vol. 1, p. 12.
8. Ibid., p. 20.
9. Ibid., p. 23.
10. Samuel Miller, *An Essay on the Warrant, Nature, and Duties of the Office of the Ruling Elder* (Philadelphia: Presbyterian Board of Publication, 1832), p. 4.
11. Ibid., p. 175.
12. Ibid., p. 194.
13. Ibid., p. 201.
14. Ibid., p. 207.
15. Ibid., p. 213.
16. Ibid., p. 214.

17. In 1984 excerpts from Miller's book on the elder were reprinted in booklet form under the title *The Ruling Elder*, by Presbyterian Heritage Publications, P. O. Box 180922, Dallas, Texas 75218. The text was made more readable by changing to contemporary spelling, grammar, and word usage. A second edition was published in 1994. This booklet is a valuable resource for understanding the significance of the office of elder.
18. Miller, *An Essay on the Warrant, Nature, and Duties of the Office of the Ruling Elder*, p. 302.
19. Ibid., p. 253.

Chapter 5. The Ordered Ministry of Deacon

1. John Calvin, *Institutes of the Christian Religion*, 4.3.9, ed. John T. McNeill, trans. Ford Lewis Battles, LCC (Philadelphia: Westminster Press, 1960), vol. 2, p. 123.
2. Janet G. MacGregor, *The Scottish Presbyterian Polity* (Edinburgh: Oliver and Boyd, 1926), pp. 108, 123.
3. *Minutes*, General Assembly, 1841, p. 418, quoted in Samuel J. Baird, *A Collection of the Acts, Deliverances, and Testimonies of the Supreme Judicatory of the Presbyterian Church* (Philadelphia: Presbyterian Board of Publication, 1856), p. 38.
4. James B. Ramsey, *The Deaconship* (Richmond: Presbyterian Publishing Company, 1879), p. 17.
5. Ibid., pp. 17–18.
6. Ibid., p. 19.
7. Ibid., p. 23.
8. Ibid., p. 25.
9. Ibid., pp. 26–27.
10. *A Proposal for Considering the Theology and Practice of Ordination in the Presbyterian Church (U.S.A.)* (Louisville, Ky: The Theology and Worship Ministry Unit, Presbyterian Church (U.S.A.), 1992), pp. 101–2.
11. Ibid., p. 102.

Chapter 6. A First Look at the Session

1. Presbyterian Church (U.S.A.), Directory for the Service of God, S-6.0200, 1983.

Chapter 9. Leading the Church in Mission

1. Directory for the Service of God, S-4.0600a.
2. See Robert McAfee Brown, *Making Peace in the Global Village* (Philadelphia: Westminster Press, 1981), p. 20.

Chapter 10. Presbytery, Synod, and the General Assembly

1. Janet G. MacGregor, *The Scottish Presbyterian Polity* (Edinburgh: Oliver and Boyd, 1926), p. 137.

Chapter 11. Stewardship, Finance, and Property

1. Directory for the Service of God, S-2.0900.
2. Ben Lacy Rose, *Confirming Your Call* (Richmond: John Knox Press, 1967), pp. 16, 17.

3. In this section we are heavily indebted to John C. Bramer, *Efficient Church Business Management* (Philadelphia: Westminster Press, 1960).
4. Ibid., pp. 76, 78.

Chapter 12. Meetings of Councils and of the Congregation

1. Sarah Corbin Robert et al., *Robert's Rules of Order* (Glenview, Ill.: Scott Foresman & Company, 1981), pp. xxxi, xlii.

Chapter 13. Preserving Peace and Purity

1. Presbyterian Mission Agency is the proposed new name for the General Assembly Mission Council to be confirmed at the 2012 General Assembly.

Chapter 14. Leading the Church in Worship

1. This chart is adapted from unpublished materials compiled by the late Dr. C. Benton Kline and dated November 30, 1989. In writing this chapter on the Directory for Worship, the authors drew on these and other such unpublished materials and are heavily indebted to Dr. Kline for his research and his generosity in sharing its fruits.

INDEX OF *BOOK OF ORDER* REFERENCES

Book of Order subsections marked with a lowercase letter (for example, 14.0701a) are not included in this index, but may be found by referring to the pages listed under the appropriate numbered entry.

The authors' citations of *Book of Order* sections are indexed; cross-references within quoted *Book of Order* sections are not.

INDEX OF TOPICS

CPSIA information can be obtained
at www.ICGtesting.com
Printed in the USA
LVOW10s1734041017

551170LV00014B/1427/P